I LOVE YOU MORE THAN...

*A Heartfelt Story of a Father and Daughter and Their
Uncommon Way of Connecting*

Tom Carmazzi and Christine Carmazzi

Renown

Renown Publishing
www.renownpublishing.com

I Love You More Than... / Tom Carmazzi and Christine Carmazzi
ISBN-13: 978-1-960236-13-5

To all those who have impacted my life with the best of intentions, from my early childhood to these years as a senior citizen, I am forever indebted. From family to friends to acquaintances, your interactions with me have molded who I am today. I would not change a thing!

This book is dedicated to those who have the courage to step into uncomfortable or uncommon relationships with the heartfelt intention to share yourself for the benefit of others.

CONTENTS

Finding the Right Words

Tom

I love Monday mornings. I look forward to them as much as others crave Friday afternoons.

Most of my Mondays start the same way: an early breakfast and a bit of exercising. Then I step into my home office for my quiet time.

My desk faces our side street. It's surprisingly active outside, even in the early morning hours—people walking, jogging, or taking their young children to school. As soothing as it is to see the neighborhood in action, I am eager to start my week by sending my daughter her Quote of the Day.

Every day, Monday through Friday, I send a Quote of the Day email to Christine. It's our daily method of keeping in touch, but it's so much more than sending a random quote or just saying, "Hi, how are you doing?" It's an opportunity to continue deepening a relationship that's been decades in the making and requires intentional effort.

The mechanical side of the email-writing process is fairly predictable. I search the internet for quotes that have inspired me, or I recall words that have stuck with me from books I've either recently read or am currently reading. Still another source of inspiring quotes is the various forms of media I periodically surf. When I find a quote I like—something I think has value and can foster conversation and dialogue—I save it.

The heartfelt side of the process is to make sure I pick something I believe will have a lasting impact on our relationship. I choose quotes that will touch Christine's heart or challenge her intellect. It's really wonderful when I can find a gem that does both.

My goal is to cite either authors familiar to Christine or impactful historical figures ranging from our Founding Fathers to Billie Jean King. I'm very intentional with my choice of authors because, in addition to strengthening our father-daughter bond, I want to confirm that, regardless of all the silliness in the world, there were and still are great leaders. After all, I began this daily ritual at the beginning of the COVID-19 pandemic. With the chaos swirling all around us, it seemed like the ideal time to start a new tradition.

What do these Quote of the Day emails look like? Let's take a look at one I sent Christine's way. As with the others, it begins with a quote:

> *Where there is discord, may we bring harmony. Where there is error, may we bring truth. Where there is doubt, may we bring faith, and where there is despair, may we bring hope.*
>
> **—Margaret Thatcher** [1]

Below the quote, I commented:

> What I love about this quote is she mentions the fundamentals of human dignity: harmony, truth, faith, hope. These words get used as taglines today; yet, when I slow down and take them in, their power is timeless. Also, the nature of these words is about connection, the heart, and lifting up.
>
> —Harmony: a pleasing arrangement of the parts
>
> —Truth: an alignment of the heart and head
>
> —Faith: a belief in what is not seen
>
> —Hope: an expectation of fulfillment
>
> I believe she chose those words very intentionally to show she was a holistic leader, and she chose them for her country—to lift them up from the despair that resided in her people at the time.
>
> It seems to me that these words are growing in importance as relationships are being impacted by the drama and technology of the day. This quote is a calling forth for me, to live into these words and honor the human dignity of all folks whom I come in contact with each day—a challenge for me and one I eagerly accept!
>
> I love you more than all the opportunities to convey and maintain dignity in all we do.
>
> *Dignity Daddy*
>
> [Note the corny sign-offs we use to provide humor in context.]

Christine's reply:

> Oh my gosh! Your connection to those words and how they are included in the fundamentals of human dignity was not an obvious link to create, but one that is undeniable!

Thinking about life, as humans coexisting on planet earth, it would be impossible for humanity to survive without a small portion of all of those things—harmony, truth, faith, and hope. In order for humans to be successful, they must get others to join along. Hence, the harmony portion. As humans, we have very scientific and creative minds, thus we're always searching for "truth," which has helped us create numerous technological and quality-of-life advances. This goes a bit hand in hand with faith—humans had to believe that progression could occur. Even if something isn't right in front of you, it can still exist. And hope, a key piece, is vital to our existence. Think about where humans would be without hope—no one would work, nor have a family, nor any friends! The world would not survive for very long at all.

I'm with you on the challenge to live into these traits. I thought I'd share—the reason my response is so late today is because we had an off-site inventory audit from 7 a.m. to 4 p.m. Our team consists of people who really prize their beauty sleep, but we all agreed to go in and get the job done early! When the group showed up, we were all a little quiet, but I started laughing and joking around. I brought high energy and positivity, and we had a blast. We are all exhausted, but I think I was integral in turning the day around.

I love you more than all of the ways we can be better people, for the good of all!

Christine's the early bird.

I love it when I succeed in finding one of these gems to share with her, one that will touch her heart and, at the same time, invite her to be a leader beyond the traditional organizational requirements. My hope for her is that she'll continue to be someone who truly touches hearts for the greater good.

When I click the little paper airplane that sails my morning message to Christine, I'm hit with two simultaneous feelings:

a sense of accomplishment at the beginning of my day and joy at the possibility of impacting my daughter's life. I used to eagerly await some reply or acknowledgment from her, but it didn't take me long to understand that my motivation was misguided and the Quotes of the Day should be for her and not reciprocal acknowledgment for me.

The *impact* is all about awareness. I believe that Christine, like all of us, has been given many gifts. The impact I want is to increase her awareness of her gifts so that she can bring them into her everyday life.

That's the plan every time I hit the send button and sit back in eager anticipation of what my daughter will find in the Quote of the Day.

Christine

The Quotes of the Day arrive in my inbox Monday through Friday pretty regularly, before I'm even awake. My dad is on Central Time, and I'm on Pacific, so they typically sit idle for a few hours, partially because I am *not* a morning person—and am convinced I never will be.

I always do a scan of my emails first thing in the morning, even when I'm bleary-eyed. And it's really funny—like, "Yep, there's Dad!" I check the time stamp, which is always mind-blowing for this not-morning person. One morning, his email arrived in my inbox at something like 3:45 a.m.! I immediately thought, "Wow, what time was Dad up today?"

For me, morning means survival mode. I've been known to send sleepy emails and texts, and I often regret hitting the send button before having my morning coffee plus some time to truly wake up. But when it comes to the Quotes of the Day, I choose not to do that. Because of my delayed morning routine, I often won't open my dad's emails until midmorning or even early afternoon. I give myself plenty of time to tend to the little fires at work and settle in for the day. The last thing I want is to rush through a quote or provide a reply that doesn't feel genuine.

I usually check those emails from my laptop at home, but a few times a week I go into the office, which is a more challenging environment for reflection. Given the close proximity to coworkers, the conference room, the sales office, and a bunch of people on the other side of the walls, it gets really noisy. It's not ideal for having a clear head and avoiding distractions.

On those days, I wait until the noise and busyness of the office die down to the point where I can pay attention and answer in a thoughtful manner. That's the most important thing about reading and replying to Dad's quotes: the awareness involved.

Dad started sending the Quotes of the Day during a grim time for everybody—at the start of the COVID-19 pandemic, when there were so many unknowns and so much fear. I was isolated from my parents. Not the ideal situation.

His emails really brightened my day. More than a text or a phone call—both of which are fine ways to stay in touch—they were thought-provoking and increased my thankfulness for my position, privilege, health, and family. I've always known Dad to be someone who is very thoughtful and who enjoys getting to a deeper level with people, so I was not shocked when these Quotes started showing up in my inbox. They were welcomed!

Now that the pandemic and lockdowns are over and life is mostly back to normal, the Quotes continue to be a great way for me and Dad to strengthen our connection, and that's why I take them so seriously. They force me to put down the distraction device that I carry with me every day and explore that day's quote.

Conversing with my dad about inspiring quotes helps me to be more mindful and present. I kind of miss them when the weekend comes along.

Tom

After weekends, there's a calmness to Monday mornings and the return of our little ritual. I find comfort and satisfaction in believing that it's going to rekindle this relationship every single week. Monday has become our reconnection day, and I look forward to it every time.

This book isn't a how-to manual. We can't provide you with all the answers. What we can do is give you a glimpse into our conversations about the many facets of life: who we are versus what we do; like-hearted discourse versus like-minded dialogue; dignified leadership versus controlling leadership; staying present versus falling prey to distractions; and, my personal challenge, sharing all of me versus being closed off by my pride.

Because, really, it's about showing my love for my daughter in a way that far outlasts the phrase or sentence written. It's about showing empathy and extending forgiveness, expressing candor and being vulnerable, remaining in dialogue when tensions rise, and listening for what's *not* said. It's about loving people for who they are, without judgment, and taking a stand for who they are even when they might have temporarily forgotten.

For me and Christine, the Quote of the Day is our unique way of maintaining those connections, so we want to offer you a few quotes to think about as you dive into this book:

> It is better to light a candle than to curse the darkness.
>
> **—William L. Watkinson** [2]

> The price of greatness is responsibility.
>
> **—Winston Churchill** [3]

> Never underestimate your ability to be a leader, even if it only means being a good dad, mom, sibling, grandparent, or friend. You may only impact or lead a single person. However, we are all connected on this planet, and the seed you plant could travel far, with untold impact to bloom and affect others.
>
> **—Ben Newman** [4]

What do those quotes mean to you? What thoughts about yourself and your loved ones do they spark? Keep them in your heart and mind as you read on.

You'll have the chance to see the connections they forged

between us, and we hope you'll find your own way to create those stronger links with the people you love.

Our Story

Tom

Growing up in Urbana, Ohio, I attended a Catholic grade school. I didn't consider myself the smartest student, nor did I try very hard. I would watch the clock at the front of the room tick the seconds away, wishing it would go faster by the minute, but it never did.

In fourth grade, I developed a stutter, and it remained a big part of my life until my sophomore year of high school. The difficulty of speech was constantly on my mind. I hesitated to talk. But, unfortunately, in a Catholic school, I was frequently asked to read at Sunday Mass, and my so-called friends responded accordingly. This turned me into a loner who wanted to control his environment to reduce the chance of stuttering.

A by-product of this time of my life was the desire to prove myself. I felt I had to earn everything. This meant I would never accept charity, such as someone trying to help by finishing my sentences. My personal goals became proving I was worth something and gaining a position of control. I tried to make everything black-and-white because gray would have required more dialogue, which meant more chances to stutter.

Another by-product was a gravitation toward numbers. I was good at math, and as my brother Joe once put it, "If you're good with numbers, there will always be a job for you." To my mind, that meant engineering or accounting, and the thing about accounting is that people always want to know how they're doing financially. They want to know the score of the game.

College led to a certified public accountant (CPA) certificate, which I felt gave me deeper credibility. Eventually, I left public accounting because I didn't like certifying someone else's work; I wanted to create my own. So I went to work for a large, publicly traded manufacturing company and was successful in hitting the numbers. I really cared about little else, because numbers were black-and-white. Gray risked exposure to words I might get stuck on.

In time, I was promoted to run a million-square-foot plant with twelve hundred machine tools and two foundries. Big place! And I was this wet-nose finance guy with zero operations experience. I greatly overvalued myself because of my capability with numbers. I simply knew what levers to pull, and I was rewarded accordingly.

At that time, I was all business. I would smile and be polite, but I stuck to short sentences and got to the point. I saw figures, not faces. I avoided relationships due to my conditioning earlier in life.

After being in my role for two years, I called a meeting with the executive committee of the union—twenty-three guys, including the president of the union, who was sitting in the back of the room. I had my charts and graphs, which to me supported an obvious course of action: we would have to lay off two hundred people.

That's when the president of the union raised his hand. "Tom, there are twenty-three people in this room," he said. "And we know you're smart. But you don't *care*."

His statement rocked me, knocked me on my heels. I just stared at him, unable to respond. He had to have seen it on my face—and he wasn't done.

"To prove my point, I want you to say the names of these twenty-three people in this room. And I'll make it easy for you—tell me their first names."

There was no way around it. No chance of backing down from the challenge. The best I could do was blurt out three names. He was right. I didn't know who they were, because I didn't care. When it came down to it, numbers were what mattered to me, not the people whose lives my decisions impacted.

I don't remember how long the rest of that meeting lasted, though it felt like hours. All I know is that, when we left that room, I looked at the president and told him, "Thank you."

That response was definitely *not* what I felt I should be saying to this man who had just called me out in front of everybody else. To this day, I consider it an act of God.

In a roundabout way, I felt like he cared about me. It was clear he cared about his people, which is why he knew there was a lot of truth in what he said. I think he was hoping it would spark an awakening in my heart.

I got home and told my wife, Deb, the story, and she was brilliant in her response.

"You know what you've got to do, don't you?"

"No, I don't. What?"

"You've got to go work in every one of those departments and get to know those people."

I rebutted, "Have you seen that place? That'll take months!"

"It doesn't make a difference. You've got to do it."

She was right, of course. Over the next three months, I worked from the core room to the foundries and through the various machining departments.

Until that meeting, I was unaware that I was going in the wrong direction. I wasn't valuing relationships and had to be told, in the bluntest possible terms, that not doing so was going to be my downfall. The president knew it, and I was beginning to see it.

I wish I could say that experience changed my life forever, but it didn't. It started my journey, but there were many miles to travel before I was noticeably different. I needed many reminders from folks who cared for me.

Deb and I didn't have children until we were in our late thirties. We had Michael, who was truly a blessing, healthy in all the ways you would want your child to be.

I was still driven to succeed at work, but there was a shift underway—though it did not happen quickly enough for my son. I know now I wasn't as present as any young boy requires his father to be.

Christine was born three years later, and I was so happy to have a son and a daughter. Christine was more assertive than Mike in her early years, very sassy and bold. Consequently, she tasted soap more than she would've liked.

After Christine was born, I knew I had to do a better job of keeping our family connected. We tried to dine together every evening so we could catch up on the day. I made sure to be home by six to participate in our family life. I'd read and tell stories to the kids before bedtime each night, frequently nodding off before they did. We would start in Mike's bed, and then I would carry Christine to hers once she fell asleep.

I was also determined to pass on a family tradition to the third generation. In World War II, my father was a member of the Tenth Mountain Division, a military unit specially trained for mountain warfare. As a benefit, he was a fantastic skier, and he passed along that skill to his three boys. I followed in his footsteps by doing the same, which kicked off many fun adventures for our family.

Christine

Growing up, I viewed my dad as my best friend, but also as my father and mentor. The best friend side of him would come out while skiing together or while doing some weekend outdoor activity, like playing basketball or tennis.

I learned to ski in upstate New York, then in the hills of Illinois, Ohio, and Wisconsin. I remember getting piled into the car in the early morning hours. I'd sleep in my pajamas the whole way to wherever we were skiing. One moment we'd be pulling into the parking lot, and the next, Dad was helping us get bundled up before we hit the slopes.

Later on, when I was in elementary school, we would go out west with my aunt and uncle and their two kids. That was kind of my first little taste of freedom because, even though we four kids would often have somewhat supervised lessons, we could go skiing without our parents. We got to test a lot of boundaries, and I think maybe that's where my love of speed came from. I was the youngest, so either I learned how to be fast or I just got left behind by the boys!

Dad and I have always shared similar hobbies and interests, especially skiing. We also love spending time in our family cabin in the summer. We share deeper interests and hobbies as well, like getting frequent exercise, watching movies, and enjoying a good meal.

Dad has always been a great listener. We could have conversations on just about anything, especially as I got older. I've always felt as though he was a present father. The father side of him showed up when I needed some tough love—as he noted earlier, I had soap in my mouth much more frequently than I would have liked. He was caring, but he didn't caretake. He expected independence from his kids.

One winter, when I was a teen, I came down with a rough case of the flu, and I hadn't been outside the house in days. In that condition, who would want to be? All anyone yearns for is a blanket and a pillow. But I needed a prescription, so I asked Dad to take me to the pharmacy to pick it up. We made it all the way there and home again successfully—and then I got sick all over the passenger seat of his car.

Part of me fantasizes Dad saying, "Christine, I'll get this cleaned up. You go inside and rest, okay?" Instead, he said, "There's a towel and some cleaning supplies inside you can use to clean that up with," as he headed back inside the house.

He was also a diligent mentor to me, which he showed by coaching my various sports teams—soccer and basketball, especially. Even though he didn't play either of those sports, he still took the time to be involved with activities I loved.

The tradition of eating dinner together continued throughout my school life. It was a rare night when we weren't all gathered around the dining table, talking about our day.

Then, of course, there were the Carmazzi Rules.

Tom

As a new parent, I wanted to instill values and expectations early on and require compliance—not very surprising given my desire for clarity. So I created the "Carmazzi Rules" and stuck a copy of them on the fridge to increase awareness. Christine and I were tickled when we recently realized it's still on the fridge to this day!

The rules are divided into a primary and a secondary list, starting with the primary:

- We do not lie.
- We keep our promises.
- We do not say dirty words.
- We are nice to others.
- We have positive attitudes.
- We do not allow others to be mean to our family members.
- We will stand united in public.
- We will give 100 percent effort in all games and sports, no excuses.
- We will strive to be the best in all school activities.
- We will attend church weekly.

There's also a set of secondary rules:

- We have good manners: "please" and "thank you."
- We clean up the messes we make.

- We do not return to the dinner table.
- We do our chores.

At the bottom, I added this "icing on the cake": following these rules would result in increased trust, personal growth, and, of course, happiness.

Christine

I was still a kid at the time, probably around ten years old, when these rules were put into effect. Not long after, there was an evening I didn't want to be part of the family dinner table conversation. I was probably just bored or something like that, so I completely disregarded what the family was in the middle of doing and got up to see what was on TV. The shocker came when I tried to get back in my seat.

"No, you're not coming back," Dad said.

"Um ... what?" I couldn't have been more surprised.

When he gestured toward the list of bullet points on our fridge, I knew that these rules were going to be in our lives for the foreseeable future.

Tom

You can see this tension between my wanting the best for my kids and my desire to turn back to the comfort of facts and figures. This tension reached its height when Mike was about to graduate from high school and I realized I really didn't know him. I knew if I didn't give myself a break from work, I would regret it for the rest of my life, so I told the owner of the company where I was working that I was leaving and didn't know when I would be back.

Fortunately, he was very understanding and honored my request. We took the kids out of school and went to Park City, Utah, for two months—a true family getaway.

It wasn't easy for me. The first couple of weeks, I didn't know what to do when I awakened before the others. I would watch CNBC or read a business periodical. I could not just be me; I had to be the businessman. That's who I had become.

Eventually, I got more comfortable not monitoring the clock and optimizing every minute. I could just be me. When I returned to work, people noted a difference in my demeanor. They said I seemed calmer, less intense. I did feel different, yet I still had much further to climb. But something had definitely changed.

Mike left for college in the fall of that year, and I shed tears as we drove away from his campus. I knew those tears were a sign of progress. My heart was opening more than even the union president could have guessed all those years ago. I would need every bit of that progress because my biggest challenge was yet to come.

Now seems like a good time to share one of our Quote of the Day emails that relates to challenging situations:

> Good Morning, Darling! So glad you made it home safely. Hope you got your bags in a timely manner.

Here is your QoD:

We are all faced with a series of great opportunities brilliantly disguised as impossible situations.

—Charles Swindoll [5]

Charles Swindoll is an evangelical Christian pastor, author, educator, and radio preacher. He founded Insight for Living, headquartered in Frisco, Texas, which airs a radio program of the same name on more than 2,000 stations around the world in 15 languages. Whoa, this guy gets around![6]

I believe this quote to be true at its core. So many times in my life, I had situations that I felt were grim, which produced wonderful learnings. The most important thing for me was to shift from victimhood to awareness. To get past the circumstance of the moment. At my most recent Bible study, one of the members was commenting on how a circumstance impacted his life. I commented that it was his CHOICE related to that circumstance that impacted his life. That our choices make our life, not the circumstances. I know it caught him off guard; he nodded his head in agreement, and yet I think he was still pondering.

For me, since things are happening all the time, it is truly how quickly I will shift away from the ego invitations of the moment to the holistic choice of the heart, then head, then hands. Also, when I am choosing things in the context of my purpose and related goals, I experience different circumstances. Proactive choices will create different circumstances.

I love you more than choices that we can make in our lives.

Choosing Carmazzi

11

Hi, Daddio!!

Yes—everything was SHOCKINGLY smooth! Thank you again for the tickets. It feels nice to be home, but I do miss you and mom already!

This is great stuff and also has a lot to say about how people handle and view stressful situations. There are folks who view impossible situations as just that, something that will never get resolved, and then you have people who view those situations as an invitation! Victimhood versus being at choice! Like you said, that big shift between awareness and victimhood says it all. That's brave and impressive of you to speak out and to share your learning.

Amen on that last sentence. Going out and getting what you want bodes much more favorably for you versus sitting back and letting the world float you along!

I love you more than all of my future that I hold in my hands!

xoxox

Proactive Carmazzi

Life Challenges and the Opportunities They Present

Christine

I've always been a bit of a homebody.

That's not to say I'm disconnected from people. I had a lot of acquaintances in my high school class of a thousand kids, mostly through the social circles formed from activities like lacrosse and Girl Scouts, not that those circles necessarily overlapped. But they were just that: acquaintances. I'm like Dad in that regard; I don't form a lot of close friendships.

When planning for college, I decided to move far away from home in Illinois. A lot of my classmates went to schools nearby in the Midwest, but I didn't want my college experience to be a continuation of high school. I wanted to start fresh.

It was way more challenging than I thought possible.

One thing I've learned about myself is that, internally at least, I tend to overpromise and underdeliver. I hype myself up. I tell myself, "You've got this!" especially in scenarios that have the potential to be incredibly stressful. Leading up to an event, I'm calm, staying mostly in my head, trying to act tough and prepared. But once I'm finally in that moment and my lifelines are gone, I sometimes crumble.

When moving away, it took everything I had to suppress my anxiety because, deep down, I knew more personal growth would occur if I moved far away from home. But it was still really rough. I felt like the proverbial fish out of water. During our introduction week at the University of Oregon, I found myself in a big icebreaker event with seventy other students, in which we went around the circle saying our names, our pronouns, and where we were from. The weird part was that I kept hearing other students say, "I'm from the Bay area." "Yeah, I'm from the Bay area."

Panic set in. I texted my mom, "What the heck's the Bay Area?"

"Do you mean San Francisco Bay?" she texted back.

"That makes sense."

And then, of course, it being the Pacific Northwest, I was expecting rain. Lots of rain. Oregon didn't disappoint, beautiful as it was. I went out and bought all new rain gear. Perfect, right?

There I was, on my way to class during a downpour, with my raincoat down to the tops of my knees and my boots up to the bottoms of my knees. My new gear worked pretty well, even if my knees themselves were soaking wet. You'd think an umbrella would have really helped, but I learned a funny thing: it seems that Oregonians don't use umbrellas. They rarely even use hoods. The sentiment is: "Oh, it's just water. It can't hurt you."

You can picture one of those funeral scenes in a movie, the overhead shot of mourners' umbrellas packed together, except in reverse—my lone umbrella holding back the rain while everybody else is bareheaded and unbothered.

So many of those little cultural things added up. The school admitted a lot of students from not just the state but the entire West Coast, which was worlds away from the Midwest. A lot of kids there came from the same high school, so it was tough to crack into social settings. My dorm suitemates were mostly locals and already had their friends.

Early socializing attempts didn't go so great. One girl and I started going on walks together. I was so excited to tell Dad. One afternoon, we stopped by a grocery store, and while I was browsing the aisles, she came up to me, whispering and furtive.

"We have to go."

"What are you talking about?" I looked around. "We just got here."

"I just stole something. We have to go."

I blinked. "You *what*?"

"My sleeve. It's already in my sleeve. We have to go *now*."

"Okay, all right."

That ended that relationship. I couldn't be friends with a shoplifter! I called Dad later and dumped the whole situation: "I only had one friend, and she turned out to be a kleptomaniac!"

I went from eating dinner with my family every evening to having meals alone in my dorm room. On the plus side, I ended up getting a 4.0 that first quarter because I didn't have much going on besides my studies. That's the opposite of what a lot of college kids experience, for sure!

But I missed my dad, big time.

Tom

I knew Christine would go to college, and I was excited that she chose Oregon—a new part of the country to explore, a good school, a place that would feed her independence. Although I knew I would miss her, I wanted to support her choice.

This sudden absence impacted me more than I expected. I was used to talking to Christine every day. Our chats were as much a part of our routine as waking up. Now she was clear across the country, and we were unable to continue our cherished routine. Sure, I had a concern that our frequency and style of communication would degrade. But I also had an apprehension that she might let her guard down when trying to make new friends with folks who did not share her values, who might influence her in face-to-face moments for the worse.

My fear was driven by being an overprotective dad, and, fortunately, it turned out to be unfounded. This became especially clear when she called me, appalled, about the shoplifting incident. Her deep-rooted values remained intact, much to my relief.

Nonetheless, when Christine left, that protective instinct went on full alert, which I did not see coming. It kept warning me that if anything were to happen to Christine way out there in Oregon, I couldn't get there quickly. My mind went to the extreme: what if there's a catastrophic event and she can't use the app on her phone that tells her how to get from X to Y? So I gave her an old-fashioned printed map with a line that I had drawn from Eugene, Oregon, to Hinsdale, Illinois, so that she could find her way home even if the electrical grid collapsed. I'm fairly certain I labeled the envelope I put it in "Emergency!"

A lot of those concerns had more to do with me than Christine. I'm the kind of guy who makes acquaintances quickly but friends very slowly. That's why Christine's leaving for college threw me for a loop. Some people might experience the loss of a friend as a two-percent reduction of their circle, but losing Christine was like removing twenty percent of my close friends. Life hadn't prepared me for such a challenge.

What had caused me to be such a guarded person? My mother was very unpredictable in her behavior. The volatile nature I observed during my childhood created an environment of distrust, so I became closed off. My aforementioned stuttering fueled my isolation. My protective shield thickened, and I trusted even fewer people.

Once I entered the business world, I was mentored by folks who believed that leaders must keep their distance so that, when they have to make tough personnel choices, they can do what's best for the business without being influenced by friendship. My childhood had prepared me perfectly for keeping my distance. I was really good at it!

Well, guess what happened. The union president who told me I didn't care about my colleagues cracked open that hardened shell, and I was left to create relationships I had been avoiding most of my life.

My trust in my kids was based on the values that Deb and I conveyed and, for the most part, modeled. I say "for the most part" because I started fatherhood very judgmental and with little tolerance, but as I matured, I wanted to hear my children's perspectives of an event rather than shut down the dialogue to demand strict compliance. I started to say, "Tell me more," instead of, "You know the consequences." I began shifting from enforcer to father to mentor.

Christine

I still have that emergency packet! The map is in there, along with some cash. And he's right; it's labeled "Emergency" in bright marker. It was a really sweet safety net for me.

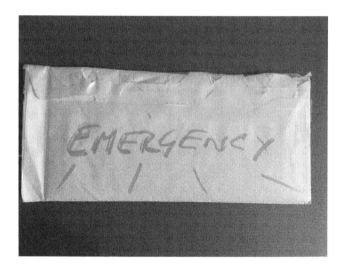

I wasn't completely out of touch with my parents while at college. We called each other periodically and had conversations I looked forward to. Every week or two, my mom would send me a letter that summarized what had happened in their lives since her last letter, or she might include a local news article. Dad would also send a card around the same time, including a photo of us or a special place we visited. Dad's cards were more about reminiscing over our time together and looking forward to time ahead.

Those letters have become keepsakes. I don't throw any of them away. I fill gallon-sized Ziploc bags with them and then put the bags in a storage bin. Once that bin fills up, they go back to my parents' place in Illinois.

Tom

It's true—those letters are like homing pigeons!

During this time, the four of us also had a group text going, which started when Mike left for college. I like to joke that it was our way of making sure he was still alive. It was a surface-level form of communication, just a sentence here or there to talk about our days and to express our love for one another. It was like a submarine's sonar pinging of a target, sending out that *ding* and hoping for a response.

These methods of staying in touch were not complex. There was a nice simplicity to them. Along with text messages and letters, Deb and I would also send cards to Christine and Mike. We'd print photos that captured a moment and use them for the front of the card, with heartfelt messages to our kids written on the inside. Simple and relational. We wanted to keep the communication impactful enough to let each one of us know just how important we were in each other's lives.

Christine

As simple as it may seem, getting mail from your family is something to look forward to. It's no fun finding only bills or coupons in the mailbox. Receiving a letter and a photo meant so much to me, even though it cost my parents just a few minutes of their time and a stamp.

The texts were wonderful reminders that I had this great family looking out for me and loving me, even from a distance. It was a reminder that, even though we were physically apart, we could be reached easily. Receiving the letters was the extra special little thing that really helped bridge that gap of spatial differences.

Even with those lifelines, I still felt lonely. Given I had no real friends for the first four months of college, I found obscure ways to fill my time. My main coping mechanism was exercise, and that definitely amped up during my freshman year. I would spend three hours a day at the gym—running, lifting weights, doing yoga, enjoying the sauna. I felt like I was making some progress in handling the solitude.

Running became an especially vital activity. There were amazing trails all around campus, and I loved pushing myself to see how far and how fast I could go, in part because I gain clarity when I run. If I'm thinking about something particularly challenging or upsetting, running is a really great way to boost my emotions. Also, exercising gave me a sense of control, a welcome feeling during the unexpected shock of my early college months.

Tom

For me, work was how I coped with Christine's absence, how I numbed my loss of her. The texts and periodic communication helped, but Deb was much better at keeping in touch with the kids, so I trusted that she would let me know if Christine were in need. Also, Christine had demonstrated that, while she was independent, she would contact me if she needed help.

Although Christine and I had always maintained a strong relationship, there were times she had to make her stand, which happened in various ways that surprised Deb and me—like the time she tried hitchhiking at our street corner, when she was six, because she wanted to leave home. During the same period, she would hide in her tree house for hours because she felt she was not getting enough attention. She also could get pretty frisky on the soccer field with other players, as well as with the referees.

As much as I wanted her to know that kind of behavior was not acceptable, I loved her competitiveness and her desire to stand for what she felt was fair. I saw in her qualities I craved as a child yet avoided due to my stuttering.

I believe that family relationships are for a lifetime and are the most impactful of all relationships. They are created when parents and children are learning and determining who they are, in good times and bad. They are instrumental in influencing the choices that mold who a person becomes.

It's an understatement to say that the births of Mike and Christine had a huge impact on my life. They were an invitation for me to mature and sand down my sharper edges.

I believe the old adage that "blood is thicker than water," but it's not about the bloodline itself. It's about the shared experiences and the related growth. My love for my children runs deeper than for anyone else. As life unfolded, I knew that our relationships would change. It's normal with things like college, marriage, and career.

Nonetheless, I was unwilling to sit on the sidelines and let our family evolve *normally*. I wanted to be very intentional about how it evolved while, at the same time, not too onerous or caretaking.

When my children left the house and the ease of proximity was removed, I knew that structure had to be replaced with something that would maintain and, hopefully, grow the relationship.

Christine

Being away at school and surrounded by people who didn't know me made it extremely important for me to reconnect to those who did know me—and not only knew me but knew me well. Funny enough, making the effort to stay in regular contact with my family, and vice versa, gave me the confidence to put myself out there. Purposeful relationships with the people I loved the most helped me form new ones. If I hadn't, I wouldn't have met a few best friends—or my husband!

As humans, we all need some level of support to continue on and move forward. No humans have ever been successful purely on their own, without any outside contact.

Family can and should be the biggest of those support systems, as well as our strongest motivator to professional and personal success. Dad's right when he says that family relationships are for a lifetime. When dissension occurs, you can't just walk away from family, no matter how hard it might be to stay. I often think back to my dad's relationship with my grandma and her manipulative tendencies and how challenging that must have been for him at times. He is the perfect example of caring for and loving a family member, regardless of the interactions, until death.

Here is a quote Dad shared with me that speaks to the challenges of life. Since we cannot avoid them, why not embrace them?

Good morning, Darling!

A wise man will make more opportunities than he finds.

—Francis Bacon [7]

This quote speaks to making your own opportunities versus waiting. My coach used to say, "Don't wait. Create!" Or, said differently, be proactive versus relying on the circumstances. The key word for me is "make." What does that really mean? For me, it is about two things: preparation and awareness.

I have to be prepared for the opportunities I create or seek. Also, I have to be aware of the opportunity when it is different from what I expect. I have to see it for what it is and how it can still lead to the desired outcome, although maybe a different path. For example, when I got my first shot at operations with Cooper Industries, it was in purchasing. I wanted a general manager role, not purchasing. However, as I pondered the role, I got excited because I was really the general manager of all the suppliers. And the learning would be much greater with all those businesses versus being a GM over one business. Guess what—it turned out great!

I love you more than all the opportunities that come to light when I am ready and looking!

Put me in Carmazzi

Hey, Pops!

Ah! How cool! There's always more than meets the eye! I love your connection to one of your first career jobs. For me, this quote made me think of our move to Riverside.* It isn't what we had wanted originally, *but* there will be millions of opportunities to make it exactly what we want! This is so exciting—it'll be a new change of pace and a new culture, both of which have numerous growth opportunities! Life is truly what we make it! I continue to resist this change, for one reason or another (denial?), but in the end, this move *does* have to happen. Now, I'm just wondering if I should rip the Band-Aid off, so to speak, and move earlier to begin the change process! Decisions, decisions!

I love you more than all of the ways we can grow more with less!

Christine is Gaining New Perspectives

*Note: My husband, Cameron, was in medical school from 2019 to 2023. Upon graduation, he learned that he would be doing his residency at a hospital in Riverside, CA—not one of his top choices. We were not too thrilled to be heading to Southern California (especially the desert!). However, we've grown to take it in stride and have found many lovable aspects of life down south.

Tom

This email exchange revealed Christine's change in perspective. Throughout the shift in our relationship during her college move, we both had to adjust to new ways of doing things. Any season of change invites us into new growth opportunities. Even with this additional wisdom, our means of keeping our close relationship experienced another radical shift as we, along with everybody else, went through the world-changing events of early 2020.

Christine

I'm inspired when I hear my dad's perspective about how he feels he always has a choice, particularly to lead his life and our family into a better path. It's a perfect reminder that there are always opportunities to put a positive light on those instances that might seem challenging or less favorable in the moment.

QUESTIONS FOR REFLECTION

When have you experienced a shift in perspective because of a challenge you had to endure? What did you learn through that experience? What became possible as a result?

Fear or Freedom?
We Had to Choose

Christine

In early 2020, I had just gotten back from a trip to San Diego with Cameron, who was my fiancé at the time. We experienced wonderful weather, great hikes, and, most importantly, amazing food! Getting away for a sunny vacation was a fantastic break from winter.

At this time, I was living and working in Eugene, Oregon, two hours south of Portland, where Cameron was in medical school. My day-to-day was relatively mundane. I'd go to work and, afterwards, either rock climb or go to the gym, make dinner or see a friend for a drink, then go to bed and repeat the next day. Cam and I often switched off weekends traveling to see each other, so I was home really only during the week and a couple of weekends a month, if that.

One morning, my coworkers and I were plugging away in our X-shaped cubicle when one of them said, "Oh my gosh, there's this new virus that's really taking hold in Asia." We started reading the article together, and I remember thinking, "Oh, jeez, this is scary." But I didn't think much past that, until some cases landed in the U. S. a few days later.

I worked in person until Friday, March 13, when I asked my boss for permission to work remotely. I packed my things and headed north to "hunker down for two weeks" with Cameron and his family. I'm so fortunate that I was able to spend that time with him and his family. It was wonderful for our mental health. I got to connect with his family on a deeper level than ever before.

Then those two weeks turned into months and months. Our adjusted lifestyle had to undergo even more adjustments. It was quite the change to go from living on my own to co-habitating with five other adults and two cats! I went from working in my apartment alone to commandeering the Colberts' dining-room table. Life was no longer about single survival. We were able to make the most of it by enjoying each other's company, even resurrecting old hobbies like playing Nintendo Wii Golf, putting together puzzles, and, of course, cooking together. Cam's entire family loves preparing insanely extravagant meals.

Underlying this incredible time of closeness with his family was a very real fear for me—not the fear of my own mortality but of spreading illness to the people I care about. I hated the idea of being sick and especially of being out of commission for that long, but it was more that I worried about my health impacting someone else's.

28

I struggle with this more than Dad does, I think. What I know is that the connection between mind and body is so much greater than we tend to acknowledge. It's our best asset and our worst enemy, all in one. I discovered that I could wind myself up to a point where I'd feel symptomatic.

It was during the COVID pandemic that I had my first ever panic attack. I had returned to my apartment in Eugene, probably for some work-related purpose. The two-hour drive between Eugene and Portland is on a beautiful stretch of the Willamette Valley, with wonderful outdoor opportunities, many of which are less crowded than the excursions close to Portland, so Cam and I would occasionally visit my apartment for a kind of mini-vacation. But on this particular occasion, I was at my apartment alone and hadn't been in physical contact with anyone for weeks. I was on a conference call, probably still mired in fearful thoughts, when I suddenly started feeling lightheaded. I felt a tightness in my chest. I had difficulty breathing. The classic symptoms of COVID. It was so bad that I threw on a mask and drove myself to the nearest testing site. Not surprisingly, the results came back negative, but all these worries kept going through my head nonstop. I had to talk myself down from thinking I had an illness I didn't actually have!

Something I discovered through COVID is that I am always at choice. Am I going to choose to be anxious and continue to let myself feel things that aren't really there? Or am I going to take control and calm myself down so I can think about what really is there? I'm not saying that we can simply choose not to be sick, but there are a lot of situations in life where the outcome can be significantly influenced by our approach.

For me, it's a work in progress, but I at least have that awareness. For example, during a recent holiday season, Cam found out he had COVID the day after he arrived at my parents' home in Chicago. I instantly got scared that I, too, had contracted the disease, and I worked myself into feeling symptoms that didn't actually exist. I started to feel lightheaded, I had a tightness in my chest, and I suddenly felt a bit hot. I know this was a result of my overreaction because, after forcing myself to go outside and go for a run, I felt calmer and more clearheaded, and those symptoms went away.

Running was the lifeline I needed to free myself from the fear, while still being cognizant of my health and the health of others. What helps me now is knowing I can choose to be in a state of fear or I can take matters into my own hands and test what is really scaring me.

Tom

Like Christine, I wasn't fearful of the disease for myself, but I was concerned for loved ones like my mother and my brother, since they were both in poor health. During the early months of the pandemic, our family was still connected, though our ability to visit each other in person was severely limited. Nonetheless, I wanted to visit my mother, so I drove three hundred miles to be present with her.

I believe that drive was when the impact of the pandemic really sank in. Roughly three-quarters of the vehicles on the interstate were semitrucks, very few cars. Commerce was moving, but people weren't.

The reality of the pandemic was also obvious in Urbana, Ohio, when I arrived. There were no church services, no dining out. It was just Mom and me, no other relatives. Mom was her usual frisky self. She was unfazed by the virus and thought there was little chance of her catching it. She was more upset that everything was closed.

This trip was also when it hit me how isolated everyone was. Although I don't have a bunch of friends, I can take only so much isolation. I do still cherish periodic interaction with those in my community, and Zoom was *not* a substitute.

On my return to Chicago, I began to think more and more of Christine. I wanted to have some way of reaching out to her on a regular basis to let her know I was still there for her and, hopefully, to provide some consistency, character, and love during a time of fear and anxiety. I had retired just a few months before the pandemic hit, so I figured this might also be a way to come off the sidelines, so to speak, and do something other than worry or feel helpless.

Inspiration for that something came from an unexpected source: a political news publication to which a friend had subscribed me. I wasn't too interested in the content of the publication, but every issue featured quotes from our forefathers or other important people that resonated with me. Quotes from George Washington and Abraham Lincoln really struck home.

Because Christine and I had been further separated by the wackiness of a global pandemic, my heart grew even more tender toward her. I wanted to provide her with something that would be grounding. Just as importantly, I wanted to show her examples of good leadership, partly because of the doubts I had concerning our country's leadership. Those first quotes I encountered were from people who had a history of providing leadership and impacting our country. I wanted to send something to Christine that conveyed stability, leadership, and character. For example, here's one from a 1916 pamphlet by a German American clergyman-turned-public speaker:

> You cannot help men [or women] permanently by doing for them what they could and should do for themselves.
>
> **—William Boetcker** [8]

Initially, I was super selective, simply looking for words that seemed impactful. I wasn't choosing a quote every day, yet within three to four months, it turned into a daily event on the weekdays. I started to research quotes that I thought resonated with the spirit of what I was trying to create. The Quote of the Day was born!

Granted, it seems like a small thing, yet in the moment, I believed that the impact would be greater than I imagined. Once I sent a couple of quotes to Christine, I really liked the feeling and wanted to have my "fix" every day—not just of providing guidance for Christine but of fostering a deeper dialogue with her. I no longer felt helpless or distant, because I was having these stronger conversations with my daughter five days a week, and it felt wonderful.

Here is one of our first exchanges:

Good morning, Darling! It's go time!

Here is your QoD:

In the end, we only regret the chances we didn't take, the relationships we were afraid to have, and the decisions we waited too long to make.

—Lewis Carroll [9]

Lewis Carroll is probably most recognized for his fantasy books *Alice's Adventures in Wonderland* and its sequel, *Through the Looking-Glass*, but he was also a poet, mathematician, photographer, and inventor. He was noted for his facility with word play, logic, and fantasy. I am not sure if we have heard from Lewy before, but I like this quote!

This sounds really familiar to me. We discussed the third point as part of the book we are reading, *Courage Is Calling*! For me, the common theme among the three is a fear or lack of courage. I hadn't attached regret to that book, and yet here it is! And it makes a ton of sense that I would have regret when I lack the courage to do things that will make me a better person. Maybe that is in the later chapters!

As I think of my life, I have experienced all three, and yet I am blessed that I have been able to recover most of the time, or see that "everything happens for a reason." Accordingly, the regret was relatively short-lived. I can think of a couple career moves that were "chances" or "waits" that I was able to achieve at a later time by initiating the dialogue to see if the opportunity was still available. And guess what—it was! That happened at Cooper a couple of times.

I love you more than all the learnings in life from stepping in versus stepping out.

Stepping Carmazzi

Hey, Pops!

This one packs a punch! What a great reminder to really live life to the fullest and not hold back! Don't hold back because of fear of loss, or what others might think of you, or your fear of not being "enough." In the end, it sounds as though we'll have more regrets as to the chances we DIDN'T take versus the ones that we did. This makes a lot of sense—when we don't take chances, doors are left open, we don't have closure, or the knowledge of what could have been. If we really go for every opportunity, if nothing more, we at least have closure and a more definitive path forward to achieving what we want.

How lucky you are that those opportunities were still there—I think that speaks more to you and your value versus the opportunity itself. Said otherwise, you created and held those opportunities because of who you are!

I love you more than all of the ways we can live life to the fullest, each day!

Christine is alive!

Christine

The first quote that arrived from Dad was a great surprise. There wasn't any question of not replying. It's not as if Dad was requiring a response to his quote and his observation about it, but I do remember thinking, "There's just so much here to unpack that I have to reply."

Dad's a very thoughtful person, too, so as I read it, I could see he had put a lot of time and care into what he had sent me. It was an invitation to go in and include my thoughts about the same quote. It developed very organically. He didn't give me a heads-up about what he was planning to do, and we didn't work out a schedule or anything like that. It just developed naturally out of our conversations.

And the quotes became a tremendous help! Those first few months of the pandemic were extraordinarily stressful. No one knew what was going on, but now I had something that was giving me consistency in a very inconsistent time. Even though I was with Cam and his family, I hated being away from my family and knowing there wasn't much I could do about that separation. The quotes helped me feel the love and connection to Dad every day that I was missing, which in turn helped keep fear at bay.

Tom

The pandemic presented me with two choices: either give in to fear and feel like a victim or take heartfelt action and remove the chains of fear. I believe this choice applies to daily life, not just to the pandemic. How many times do I allow fear to imprison my actions or values? Too many! However, when I take responsibility for my thoughts and actions, I have the freedom to pursue a life that is fear*less*.

One aspect of fear I've grappled with is the victim-villain-hero triangle. For the triangle to work, you've got to have a victim, a villain, and a hero. When I first learned of this dynamic, I was, in my own view, the hero, and I was addicted to playing that role. I would find people who considered themselves the victim, and I would save them from their villains. The truth be told, sometimes I would fabricate the villain to feed my addiction. Finally, I realized I was not saving anyone; I was actually hindering their growth! Did this realization cause me to change overnight? Heavens no! I was overcome with fear because if I was not the hero, then who was I? Over time, I learned that my fear was unfounded. I actually had more choices to help people genuinely when I stepped out of the triangle!

I have learned a lot about fear. One result of fear is that we often make assumptions that aren't true. Look at the stuttering I struggled with until I was sixteen years old. You would think, given the way I speak now and the business successes I've had, that the fear is long gone. I wish I could say that I'm no longer haunted by the fear of stuttering, but I can't. Just last week, I was presenting to about two hundred folks, and the thought crossed my mind, even though the possibility of my stuttering hasn't existed for decades.

If I limit myself because of this fear of stuttering, I'm going to show up much differently to others and even to myself. But I've found that telling myself that's no longer who I am creates remarkable freedom—I'm not a victim. By the same token, I'm not a hero, and I'm not a villain. I have chosen to step off the triangle and take personal responsibility!

With my fear set aside and freedom embraced, I realized that the Quotes I was sharing with Christine were no longer about the pandemic. They were about character, caring, love, and life that transcend any specific disease or event. They were about our relationship, which will last a lifetime. The pandemic was a catalyst, a call for me to be a better father, but the Quotes were primarily about deepening that relationship and, just as importantly, developing a consistency out of which to do that.

Even without a crisis like COVID, there are still daily challenges that require maintaining those connections—immersion in social media, numbing with drugs and alcohol, obsessing over work while at home—all resulting in an emotional absence. The Quotes are a simple little tool that provide Christine and me with a basic structure for sharing our perspectives on a given topic.

Said differently, maintaining relationships is about exploring perspectives without judgment. It requires vulnerability as well. In these communications with Christine, I'm telling on myself and some of the silly choices I made throughout my life and the consequences of those decisions.

That doesn't mean it's restricted to fathers and daughters, or fathers and sons, or even family. For example, if something tragic were to happen and I found myself without close family, this framework could be used with any friend. If I were to send one of my friends a quote and my commentary over the next couple months, just like I've done with Christine, I truly believe that we would deepen our relationship in a similar manner.

Christine

Think of it this way: there are eight billion people on this planet now, but funny enough, true relationships are, in many ways, growing scarcer while, on the other hand, becoming easier than ever to create. Changes are occurring at lightning speed, which makes it difficult for people from different generations to truly relate to each other.

This makes the family unit so vital and unique. If you have nothing else in common, you at least share the same genes. If your relationship with your family isn't solid, then you're missing a foundational piece in life. Everyone has differences, no matter their friends or family. But really leaning back on this family unit, this camaraderie you share with no one else in the world, means you're truly linked.

It's crucial to find any excuse to strengthen that link, which is what the Quotes do for me and Dad. We can lean on each other in troubling times and really discuss the things that matter most in life.

The pandemic drove our appreciation for those things we had lost, but it doesn't have to be the only eye-opener. If you have a relationship that you wish you could strengthen, then let that be your catalyst for deeper connection. We don't have to wait for a crisis. The opportunity is always there.

QUESTION FOR REFLECTION

When you look beyond the fear of the moment to the possible freedom of the future, what opportunities do you see for your life?

I LOVE YOU MORE THAN...

The Courage to Address
Hot-Button Topics

Tom

The Quotes of the Day started as my way of maintaining and deepening my connection with Christine, but I realized that it couldn't just be me giving her a quote and then spoon-feeding her the lesson. I was intentional in highlighting an attribute of leadership, yet many times not naming that attribute. I felt that if I did, it would seem like I was preaching, which absolutely was not the goal. Plus, I find that telling a personal story in a particular context shows vulnerability and increases the impact because it is real, whether I was successful or not.

I wanted to encourage Christine in her leadership because it is a major interest of mine. Rather than talking about a specific person, I would touch on attributes that may be relevant to the story, without pointing fingers. Why? I'm not a fan of gossip, and once I start bringing specific people or positions into play, I run the risk of losing the bigger message: the role of leadership in our daily lives. Learning about leadership provides pearls that can be cultivated again and again. If I reference a specific person, leadership lessons live only in the context of that person.

For me, one of the attributes of leadership is the ability to discuss controversial topics respectfully. I've mentioned how I don't have many close friends. When a debate or contentious dialogue with someone who is not one of my few friends goes south, it's really of little concern to me. Fortunately or unfortunately, that's how I behaved much of my business career, as a guy who saw figures instead of faces.

However, with Christine, I was afraid of losing one of my few close friends if I ventured into a new topic on which she might have a strong opinion. Christine tends toward liberal political and social views, whereas I lean conservative. I'm one of those guys who believes that well-intended capitalism has significant benefits and we should let companies compete in a free market that will, over time, determine which companies are serving humanity the best. Granted, I am well aware that too many companies let greed get the best of them.

As I step into dialogues with Christine about topics like climate change and Black Lives Matter, I know she takes a different perspective. My goal in those dialogues is to listen, learn, and model constructive debate rather than to dictate opinion. And yet, knowing that's not my strength, I worry that my ego will damage our relationship, possibly beyond repair.

Black Lives Matter proved to be one of those hot-button topics. It was a very sensitive topic for me. I felt that the organization had preyed on the emotions of the moment and used them for its own agenda and to gain power. I emphasized the harm in labeling or generalizing entire ethnic groups based on a few outliers. In my view, the criticism aimed at the United States over the past three years has been very unjustified and destructive, with its impact greatly outweighing the damage caused throughout our nation's history. I'm not condoning unjust actions of the past, but I want "liberty and justice for all," not the vocal few.

Christine

This was a hard topic for us to tackle, but my goal during these conversations wasn't to change my dad's mind. I wanted to provide a perspective that he probably hadn't seen or heard before.

Like him, I value justice, honesty, and integrity—qualities I felt some members of police forces around our country were not abiding by. I recognized my privilege in never having experienced the pain and suffering Black Americans have, yet I could empathize with their situation. Given that I had never been directly impacted by police brutality, I felt it wasn't my place to say how one group should protest. That was for them to decide, regardless of whether I viewed it as right or wrong. It was not my place to judge.

I couldn't imagine having a loved one killed by police, and I hoped I would never have to go through that. I didn't disagree with Dad that, in a general sense, all lives matter, but the Black Lives Matter movement was hyper-focused on Black people for a reason: they were experiencing disproportionate police brutality compared to other racial groups.

My dad and I found pieces of each other's arguments that we could resonate with, but I believe we still have opposing viewpoints. The great part is that, because of the way we approach our conversations, opposing viewpoints aren't the end of the world. Challenging each other's preconceived notions doesn't have to end with us getting into an argument, and the way we talk about them prevents that.

I'm definitely not the kind of person who seeks debate. I think it depends on whom I'm talking to. I usually don't like to debate if I'm in a group setting, because I don't really know how my audience is going to react. But with people I feel more comfortable around, I think that a debate can be healthy. It's a conversation, an exchange of ideas. The more opposing viewpoints someone can hear, the better, especially when it's not coming from a need to come out on top.

I typically surround myself with pretty like-minded people. But at my first job after college, I ran into a situation with a coworker who would say things just to rile everyone else up.

One day, completely out of the blue, he says, "I'm being marginalized."

I frowned and said, "What are you talking about?"

"Because I'm a white male who owns a gun."

What in the world? I couldn't quite believe it. He said this in a corporate setting to an audience of nearly all liberal white people, packed together in cubicles. I couldn't understand his intention. What was he trying to get across? What was he trying to bring about?

He just wanted to argue. It's a trap I've learned to avoid, so I simply said, "Listen, this is where I stand, and I'm done talking about this. I have no intention of picking it up further." I recognized that he was not listening and just wanted to get a reaction from people. That's not a dialogue, and that's not how viewpoints get heard and acknowledged.

Everyone has different opinions on many topics. Unfortunately, I feel as though encountering someone with opinions that are different from ours is becoming more challenging and more personal. We've got this idea that it's about winning or about right versus wrong, and that ruins good, honest conversation.

Tom

When it comes to having those honest conversations, a big concern I have—and a reason I shy away from intense debate—is whether I'm basing my opinions on accurate information. As I step into a dialogue and share what I know, I don't want to present false or faulty data. I remain hesitant to get into aspects of things that are beyond what I have personally experienced. Even then, my knowledge can be limited. I've got a pretty good financial background, yet there are parts of the stock market and insurance products that are way out of my depth.

I now avoid debating for debate's sake. Early in my career, getting into a dialogue was about winning. I know what that feels like and where it ends up. It was much more damaging to me because people didn't want to be around me. They didn't like getting verbally beat up all the time.

I had a longtime coach—Therese Kienast, Master Certified Coach—who was good at steering dialogues to places I didn't want to go. Periodically, our conversations would get heated. Emotions would run high. My words became judgmental. I would ask for a break, not as avoidance or flight, but honoring the relationship above the "tension of the moment," as Therese would call it.

This action helped to ensure that I didn't create a situation from which the relationship was irretrievable.

Now contemplating how and why I step into dialogues is a fundamental facet for me. Am I doing so simply to convince or persuade? Or am I doing so with curiosity, truly believing that I'm going to learn something? Although Christine and I are similar in many ways, we differ so much in other ways that I know I can benefit from her perspective.

If we're discussing a leadership topic or how to navigate challenging situations, I will weigh in with my perspective. I do so by sharing my experiences, offering them as a potential, but not mandatory, guide.

I find courage through the trust I have in Christine. Plus, each time I engage in a challenging conversation with her, the next time becomes easier. Granted, we have a long history together, but that does not mean we have shared everything. Moreover, I believe it's my responsibility as her father to model stepping into dialogues that may be scary.

Christine

Dad nailed it! We have this trust with one another that allows us to share things without judgment, and we know we'll listen to what each other has to say. This trust hasn't happened overnight, and it was built up by each new challenging conversation. Dad's never given me a reason to believe that he won't be respectful or reasonable when I share my thoughts, and I try to reciprocate when he has an opposing viewpoint.

Too often in our world, we tune out opposing thoughts. We instantly shut down the idea that someone with a different view might have a valuable perspective. This has created a massive divide between people in our nation, one that could be the downfall of our society.

I love my dad, and I always will, and knowing that we have differences is something I view as a benefit, not a weakness.

Tom

My concern about the potential for damaging relationships drove me to be what others have called a "feedback junkie." I wanted to know if I was doing a good job in preventing that damage, so I started asking folks to provide me with feedback, for which I used a simple structure. What does this look like in terms of practical application? For several years now, I've been asking Christine to give me what I call "Keep, Stop, and Start" feedback—things I should *keep* doing, things I should *stop* doing, and things I should *start* doing.

The first time I asked Christine to use this process, I was afraid of how she might respond. It's one thing to ask coworkers and employers for feedback, but asking for feedback from family members is at a whole new level. What if they told me I'm an idiot or a self-centered jerk or—fill in the blank. That would really hurt, regardless of the validity. And Christine knows me better than most everyone else on the planet, so if she were to level a hefty critique at me, my reaction would be: "Oh, wow, that's probably true." Was I ready for that possible outcome? When I take the risk and ask her for that critique, it's because I want to be a better parent, and she's got a perspective no one else has.

Christine

Dad's been asking me these sorts of questions for probably a decade, since I was in my late teens. They're never like a surprise test or anything like that. Usually, it's something he gently inquires after we've spent time together.

On one of our skiing trips out West, toward the end of our last days together enjoying the slopes, Dad asked me, "Okay, what's something I should keep doing? What's something I should stop doing? And what's something I should start doing?" When he asks these kinds of questions, he's opening himself up to receive fresh and honest feedback from me, and I value that trust because those are times when it's usually just Dad and me, zero distractions. There's time to focus.

It's actually really nice to hear the person you look up to and who's charged with taking care of you asking, "What is something that you wish were different about me?" Or, "Do you understand why I handled that situation the way I did?" Dad's showing his love by expressing vulnerability, in that he's trusting me to share what I'm really feeling with him.

It's not as if I have a ready list of criticisms for him. I'm trying not to be the person who holds on to things for a long time. So, if there is something Dad does that I want to critique, it's not like I keep it on a shelf in the back of my brain, dust it off, and say, "I've been waiting for you to ask me! Here it is!"

Tom

Not too long ago, I sent Christine the following Quote of the Day email, starting with a quote often attributed to Pope Paul VI:

All life demands struggle. Those who have everything given to them become lazy, selfish, and insensitive to the real values of life. The very striving and hard work that we so constantly try to avoid is the major building block in the person we are today.

The Pope is making his stand for hard work and "stepping into the arena." What I find interesting in this quote is the word "avoid." He is saying we avoid what helps us grow. It is as if we are wired to gravitate to the comfort zone, and yet that is where, over the long term, we become less comfortable.

I had not thought of the comfort zone in terms of duration. I believe going there for rest and recovery is very needed. However, when I stay there, I begin to atrophy— mentally, physically, and emotionally. And the falsehood that staying there brings comfort is exposed sooner or later by physical pain due to inactivity—mental and emotional decline due to isolation from new friendships and challenges.

In this context, there is a word I would change: struggle. I prefer challenge. I get excited for challenges, not for struggles. Granted, there are many of life's events that start as possible struggles, like the loss of a loved one, but if I reword that to be a challenge or an opportunity for growth and maturity, I feel different. I am still sad, but it is as if there was a reason for the loss. When I am struggling, it seems very personal, with no end in sight. Whereas, when I am challenged, it seems like an opportunity for growth as a result of this passing. And I do feel that the passings of Dad, Mom, and my brother Joe were a calling forth for me to mature further and carry forth their legacy.

I love you more than all the growth the challenges of life present.

Challenged Carmazzi

Watch how Christine picked up on it right away. That's the moment that always brings me joy!

Hey, Daddio!

What a jam-packed quote we have today. Filled with so much wisdom, too. Let's take one of the most basic forms of life—plants. Imagine all of the struggle and challenge they must endure just to grow! We, too, experience struggles to get to adulthood.

I, like you, think there's a necessary balance between being comfortable and being challenged. If we were in the constant state of challenge, we'd get burnt out quickly and maybe never return to the growth state. On the contrary, like you mentioned, if we're always comfortable, we never grow or learn.

The Pope spoke of something so true—we avoid struggles more than most things in life. Our bodies seem to be hardwired for it. I know when I'm struggling or out of my comfort zone, my body can get physically hot and uncomfortable. Those feelings are not any that I seek out on a daily basis! Just as you pointed out, my words here are very *personal*, yet we all go through them. I like how you reframed this struggle to "challenge" instead. It's as if there's something to win or gain at the end of a challenge, but at the end of struggle, there's more comfort or even a reverting to the status quo. You went through some incredibly hard times with the passing of your family, and I admire how you've stepped forward and used their passing as a reason to better yourself. I'm sure it would have been much easier for you to resort back to comfort instead.

I love you more than all of the challenges that lead to growth!

Christine is Focusing on Progress

Once again, I have been blessed with very helpful, respectful feedback. It's really about having the courage to step into a controversial topic with the ones we love most. I found the courage when I decided that the benefits of further deepening the relationship far outweighed any hits to my personal pride. In essence, I had to ask myself whether or not I was all in when it came to growing my relationship with my daughter.

Once the answer came back a resounding *yes*, the initial step became much easier to take.

QUESTIONS FOR REFLECTION

How have you addressed difficult dialogues? How did you do with putting your ego and agenda on the sidelines? What worked? What would you do differently?

The Impact of Pride and Ego on Conversations

Tom

Let me paint a familiar scene: one person engages another on a challenging topic, and both people start out by making cogent points from the point of view each sees as correct. Then one person gets fired up. Comments grow personal. Replies get heated. Emotions become heightened. The next thing we know, the two people—colleagues or friends or even family members—storm away from each other.

It's hard to step back and keep our emotions in check. And I'm not always great at following my own advice. Not long ago, I was waiting for an interviewer to call me for a podcast. When he finally did, there was so much background noise that I had to repeat myself. What was he doing, anyway? It took me a minute to realize that he was walking while he was talking, which explained the bobbing of the camera view—very distracting visually.

He ended his commute in a coffee shop, which might be where a lot of people do their work, but interviewing me there was just distracting. I told myself, "This guy doesn't care about me or about doing a great job. He was simply checking off the boxes." I had no way of knowing if my assumption was true, but my irritation turned the fantasy into reality.

The podcaster then asked me a vague question that indicated he was not prepared. I couldn't help it. I frowned at the screen. "Is this really still a good time to do this? The way in which you want to conduct the interview is not acceptable. It's just not going to work."

That was all in the first two minutes. We decided to cancel the interview and not reschedule it. He revealed in closing that his normal podcast setup was not available because he was in the middle of a move and this was the best he could do.

I knew as soon as we were done that I'd failed in three important ways. First, I didn't test my assumption as to the source of his unexpected interview style. Second, I had overreacted and taken his lack of preparation personally, making me irrevocably biased. Third, I hadn't prepared myself well for the call, either, as I was in the middle of something and so wasn't fully present when we started.

What were the consequences of my poor decisions? I learned that some of my patterns were still strong and that when I enter conversations with new acquaintances, I need to be present and curious, or else the impact will be predictable: my ego and pride will scuttle the relationship from the start.

Christine has helped me be better through our dialogues. One of our most recent discussions was on abortion, a hot-button topic if ever there was one. Even though we both tried to make a stand for what we believe, we didn't raise our voices. When things became passionate, we didn't storm off to our rooms. We talked our way through it. We have to, because preserving the relationship must be paramount.

Christine

I wouldn't trade our relationship for the world! For me, including critical thought in a conversation means removing emotion. It also means taking outside perspectives into account before picking loyalty to one side of an argument. You've got to be prepared to change your viewpoint once you hear new information or encounter an opinion different from your own.

Critical thought is essential for having an in-depth conversation. Without it, how are you supposed to have a functioning dialogue? How are you supposed to converse like two rational grown-ups if you're not reining in your emotions? Dad pointed out that bias invites debates, which is not the same as dialogue. We all have biases, which are extremely hard to change. However, quieting our biases while in discussion is key because it opens the door to having those biases tested and maybe even converted. We never know when we might realize that it's time to change our minds.

When done right, this can have a tremendous impact. I have a colleague who is very passionate about sustainability. He'll actually save all of the packaging that arrives on food products or household items, most of which comes without a clear guideline of whether it is recyclable. He'll stockpile this waste until he has a moment to research what to do with it. He even asks his kids to bring home any waste they accumulate at school.

The company I work for is very conscious of its impact on the world, and we currently have an overarching goal to remove plastic from our packaging products. This colleague has expressed his opinion that simply removing plastic is not a viable solution, as some products that replace plastic could have their own negative impacts. He and I have debated back and forth on this topic, yet we're respectful, never badmouthing one another or making assumptions about what the other person believes. We listen to each other. This has strengthened our relationship and has provided each of us with a fresher perspective than we had when we started the conversation, which means that we can work better together at solving complex, systemic issues regarding overconsumption.

I think that my conversations with Dad are so productive for a few reasons. There's the trust we have because we're confident in our love for one another and we've shown that we won't attack the other over differing opinions. Respect goes hand in hand with that trust.

The Quotes of the Day have helped us get to the healthy point we're at now, but we've hit bumps along the way in terms of challenging conversations. That doesn't mean we give up or stew in our respective corners. We have to eliminate egos. We have to give the other person a chance.

These conversations have become templates, so to speak, for how I handle difficult dialogues with others. Since my exchanges with my dad offer such a good example of how to have a productive discussion, I'm able to use that framework with those around me. Having a productive conversation without ego or emotion takes additional effort of thinking before speaking or reacting.

It's been a process full of hard lessons to learn. When I began my previous job, I was kind of thrown into the mix without a lot of background knowledge and was just expected to run with it. On one occasion, we ran out of a type of malt that our brewer needed. I dug through our Rolodex of alternatives and came up with what I thought was a solution: "Hey, could you substitute this?"

The brewer snapped back, "That's not possible," without any further clarification. He was clearly upset and frustrated and, in the middle of those emotions, didn't provide any direction or collaboration we could use to solve the problem.

Our conversation was the straw that broke the camel's back. I had made mistakes with him before, and he'd been difficult to work with then. So this confrontation wasn't unforeseen, but I perceived it as him wanting to rub it in my face and not really help. I went to the restroom, locked the door, sat on the floor, and cried.

Then I called Dad to ask, "What do I do? This guy is really just testing. How can a mistake just be punished like that?"

"Well, you'll need to talk to him face-to-face," Dad calmly urged. "You need to get him in a room. This needs to stop being over the phone and email. Find a time you can speak together and hash things out."

I sent the brewer an email apologizing for my mistake, but I added that I felt a further explanation was needed to get us back on track. I tried my best, but he was evasive, never able to find time because of his busy schedule.

He eventually left the company, but animosity from the rest of his team lingered. They felt I should have better known what to do, whereas I felt I needed more support from the team to be successful. It's one of those things I still think about. What could I have done differently? What can I learn from that failure? It has encouraged me to find better ways to engage in dialogue and apply the framework Dad and I use to defuse those situations.

Tom

When it comes to encouraging critical thinking, the process of preparing the Quotes of the Day is an immense help. I make sure I'm in the right headspace when I settle in to work on them. It's a matter of calmly selecting the quote, then investing time to flesh out my intended message. I check to see if it's missing anything or if any part of it might come across as too preachy. The final step is to type out my message with clarity so that Christine won't mistake what I'm trying to say. I'm in my element, that's for sure—in full control of what I'm doing with my thoughts and emotions.

58

Once I get a response from Christine, I can rely on our shared history to create the respectful foundation we need to continue the conversation. And beyond that, I'm genuinely curious about her perspective. Given whatever topic we're dialoguing on, I'll prepare accordingly by testing my assumptions. But since it's Christine we're talking about, these steps are second nature for me because of the depth of love and trust I have for her. We know we can be ourselves because we've done it before and have demonstrated that we can handle deeper conversations without flying off the handle from an emotional perspective.

This, of course, looks different when I'm dialoguing with others, because odds are that I don't know them as well. I'm the guy with fewer but deeper relationships, as you'll recall. The amount of practice I have with others correlates to the depth of the relationship—more practice, more depth.

What do I mean by *practice*? I prepare for the dialogue, which allows me to trust my behavior in the moment. Do you remember how poorly I handled my interaction with the podcaster? I leapt into the call without preparation. Therefore, I couldn't trust my control of my ego, and in hindsight, the outcome was predictable.

One of my worst triggers is when someone conveys a lack of respect for me or others, which I'm pretty sure originates from my childhood experience with stuttering. Grappling with the inability to speak well left me hyperaware of the amount of respect others showed me. When I don't receive the level of respect I think I'm owed, the cortisol rushes in, and I have to choose either fight or flight. Unfortunately, as we've seen, I mostly go with fight.

If I had prepared better for the podcast interview by maintaining curiosity through my intentional focus instead of multitasking, I know that the outcome would have been different.

Several years ago, I had to ask a long-term mentor to leave our company. I had to prepare for the conversation by remaining present in the moment without distractions and staying curious about his perspective.

His reaction, as you might imagine, wasn't good. He became very aggressive and angry, going so far as to accuse me of being not only a hypocrite but a liar, too. That's *not* something I take lightly, and if I had gone into the conversation with guns blazing, with no preparation as to what I might say or how I might respond, I'd have reacted poorly.

But I forced myself to remain calm and stay focused. I asked questions to clarify where we were in the dialogue. Although he left the company, we have managed to remain friends to this day, and probably at a deeper level than we were before he left. I chalk that up in part to how I handled that unenviable conversation. If I'd snapped back, that could have irreparably damaged the relationship, something I by no means wanted.

When I'm entering into a dialogue, it's important for me to remember to govern what I'm going to say. I believe that remaining objective, testing assumptions, and doing my homework on a given topic of dialogue truly help promote deep conversations. That may sound formulaic or unemotional, but it creates trust and builds credibility. It also puts people at ease. When I am in dialogue with someone who has researched a given situation and who shares his or her findings in a way that appears to be thorough, my curiosity and respect increase.

Not long ago, I touched on this subject by sending Christine a quote from one of our most impactful presidents.

Good morning, Darling!!
Here is your QoD!

Tact is the ability to describe others as they see themselves.
—Abraham Lincoln

Abe is at it again!

I would put this in the category of providing feedback. Tact adds the additional dimension of sensitivity. What I love about this quote is the idea that when I provide feedback for people, I am simply providing clarification of what they already know about themselves. For some reason, they need to hear a description of themselves from an external source. In a leadership development session my company conducted back when I was working, we had an exercise in which everybody received feedback. After that exercise, almost everyone indicated they could take more candid feedback.

I believe folks crave and need feedback. It helps them grow. I know it helps me grow. I may not like the confirmation of who I am being. Yet, I am thankful.

Two more things: There is a difference between tact and candor. Tact has sensitivity; candor is frank and direct. I believe folks appreciate the sensitivity. I know I do.

> Second, I believe it is also important to provide positive feedback tactfully. Many times, this feedback is deflected with humor. It takes tact to be sensitive and ensure it is received.
>
> I love you more than the power and lifting up of tactful feedback.
>
> *Tactful Tommy*

Christine's response showed me that she was taking our conversation to heart and digging deeper into the meaning of what I wanted to share.

> Hi, Dad!!
>
> Good morning!!
>
> Oooh—this is really cool! I had to look up the definition of tact. I like your connection to the leadership development class. It's an eye-opening experience, and the spirit of it is to give the listener a point of view about how they are perceived by others, right off the bat. The exercise isn't successful if people aren't honest!
>
> I'm similar to you in that truthful feedback can be challenging to hear in the moment, but in the long term, it's extremely beneficial (if it is coming from a credible source). We all have biases, especially about ourselves and our impact on the world. There's no way that we can truly have the full picture without external input.
>
> Lastly, I like your comment about how it can be a challenge to accept positive feedback, without adding in humor or deflecting. This makes me think of a night out with friends I had a few months ago. A friend had just been promoted at work. His coworkers he was previously close with had seemed to "ghost" him. He was letting those insecurities fill his thoughts. In addition, he began wondering if he was capable of performing his new job.

I told him that there's a reason he's in that new role, above all other candidates, and even though it's scary, it's ok to fail or make mistakes early on—it's all part of the learning process. I told him that he is very capable, intelligent, and thoughtful and that I know he will be successful. He tried to deflect, but I asked him to just step away and try to acknowledge his work and efforts that got him to where he is today.

I love you more than all of the power that words hold!

Christine's Seeking Feedback

The last piece required for having in-depth conversations is vulnerability, which builds trust. And through that trust, we're willing to share more of ourselves than we would otherwise. I can tell you that I don't have all the answers, that I do get scared, and that I do have weaknesses that hinder me throughout the day. When I reveal these weaknesses to others, it opens the opportunity to go deeper in relationships. In-depth conversation is fostered in an environment where we're honest about our shortcomings. In his book *Lead Like It Matters*, pastor and author Craig Groeschel writes, "People would rather follow a leader who is always real than one who is always right."[10] The same can apply to in-depth conversation. When we are real, we are able to expose the heart of the matter.

QUESTION FOR REFLECTION

What becomes possible for you when you put away your pride and ego?

I LOVE YOU MORE THAN...

Leading with Your Heart

Tom

I have a tiny hourglass in my home office. It hasn't seen much use since I retired, but there was a time when it was how I kept everything and everyone on a tight schedule.

There was enough sand for three minutes. Early in my career, when someone walked into my office, I would turn the hourglass over and say, "You've got three minutes to get to the point and tell me what you want."

I wish I were kidding. The timer would sit between me and this person, the sand spilling lower and lower. That's how much I desired to be in control. It was one of the first things I had to cast aside so I could truly be present, an attribute I've worked on for decades. And on a scale of 1 to 10, I might now be a solid six.

There came a time when I knew I had to stop trying to be in control and instead focus on the importance of the relationships around me.

I had a lot of work to do on myself from the get-go. As a parent, I was definitely less of a leader and more of a controller, a characteristic likely stemming from my childhood desire to control events around me to avoid being hurt. It manifested in things as basic as Christine's school sports. I wanted Christine to play basketball because I knew it would make her stronger both mentally and physically to prepare her for the challenges ahead. My incorrect assumption was that because she was a girl, she'd be weaker and, therefore, needed to get toughened up on the basketball court. I don't think I ever asked her if she *wanted* to play; instead, I kept pushing her in that direction. She did well and was tough, as I hoped she would be, but in hindsight, I don't know if she would have played if I hadn't gotten intimately involved.

Here's the thing about my controlling nature: I didn't even question it. It never crossed my mind. I automatically rationalized it as the best path forward and didn't consider input or counsel. If I knew what was best for me, then surely I knew what was best for my children; therefore, no discussion was necessary. Now granted, at some point Christine might have said that she wanted to play basketball, but I certainly don't think I asked from the heart. If I did ask, I assume I would have phrased the question in very leading manner, such as, "You love playing basketball, don't you?"

Once I am in a controlling perspective, all interactions lead to my desired outcome. I listen less and preach more; I dialogue less and assume more. And I play the "hero" more. In some way or another, I am attempting to mold other people to my agenda versus letting them live out who they are. Worded differently, I'm recreating them to be more like me.

At some point during my professional life, I realized this wasn't the way to live, always seeking control rather than modeling a leader-like example for others to follow. I was starting to make a shift at work, probably not long after my gut-wrenching confrontation with the union president about my attitude, in his words, of not caring about others. But the change was still in its early phases. I was rough around the edges.

Funny enough, my parenting skills improved as I applied strategies I was learning at work from the new culture we were creating. Do you recall the victim-villain-hero triangle I touched on in a previous chapter? I realized I had a desire to play the hero by rescuing perceived victims from their supposed villains. I'd bring home my awareness of that tendency to see if it showed up in my interactions with my family, and if it did, I would work to get myself out of it.

My efforts went in reverse, too. When I experienced successes in being a more open, more attentive husband and father who listened and asked questions instead of dictating, I took those perspectives and approaches back to the office so I could deepen my work relationships. I shared stories of using the tools I employed at home with my coworkers to strengthen them as well.

There was not a miraculous transformation but a slow, steady process, as with so many other things in life. Little by little, I changed who I was—for the better, I hoped.

Christine

Dad has definitely changed as a leader, both in our family and in our relationship, to one who is more focused on leading with his heart than needing to be in charge. This change shows up most obviously in the frequency of the questions he now asks. That might not sound like leadership to you. Aren't leaders supposed to make grand statements or proclaim the next steps?

That's not the case. It's back to control again. Dad rarely, if ever, controls conversations, or even wants to talk about himself. He's always asking thoughtful questions to deepen the relationship instead of telling me what I should do or how I should behave.

My most recent example of seeing how my dad has made a vast transformation of leading with his heart has to do with my decision to tell him about my tattoo. Last summer, three days before my wedding, I was visiting my parents in my hometown of Hinsdale. I announced that I was going for a run, and as usual, Dad asked if he could ride his bike alongside me. During the last little stretch of the run, while huffing our way up the only hill on our route, Dad asked me if I would ever consider getting a tattoo. Through my labored breaths, I said something like, "Um, I'm not sure."

When we returned to the house, we cooled off on the back porch, and after a few minutes of talking, I noticed how absent-minded I was. I couldn't stay present or focus on the conversation my dad was trying to have with me. I could only think about how I needed to tell him I already had a tattoo.

Having grown up with him as my dad and knowing the rules of our household since I was a kid, I suspected that he would not be happy about my tattoo, yet I knew I had to tell him. We just don't keep those kinds of secrets.

I braced myself for Dad's response, but he was kind, composed, and curious. He asked me questions about what I'd picked and why I'd made the decision. The conversation put to rest all my worries. I believe that if I had told him earlier in our relationship, it might have gone differently—as in, Dad laying down the law! I was fully expecting him to react in a more heated manner, yet he was very calm and respectful.

But it's about more than words. Dad's also put a lot more toward spending time with family. This doesn't necessarily mean taking trips together. It can manifest through the littlest and yet best of moments. When I come home to visit, I'll often go for a jog through the neighborhood. More often than not, like on the tattoo run, Dad will drop whatever he's doing and ask if he can ride beside me on his bike. It extends the time we have together and opens the door for even more conversations. Even if we don't talk, we still get to do the things we enjoy side by side without the words. Leading with his heart has given my dad and our family more opportunities to grow and thrive in our relationships.

Tom

I was learning how to be a better leader for my family. But what exactly is a leader? What does that person look like? I think many people confuse leader with a far different term: manager.

A manager, to me, is a person who's focused on the task and not the relationship. From my perspective as a manager at a manufacturing company, the role physically relates to a task, such as getting shipments out the door to hit the daily or monthly target. The manager makes sure the workers have the tools they need to reach those numbers. Gone are any excuses. Just make it happen. It really was more of a command-and-control kind of thing, and because of that, it was very black-and-white, which I liked.

This touches on my disregard for people, which I hadn't realized at the time. I didn't think I had to worry about the personal side of things. You've got a cold? Something's happening at home? Well, as my mom used to say to me, "Tom, if you want an excuse, you'll find one."

A leader approaches the same matters from an entirely different standpoint. Some might say that those who lead from the heart are just nice people who want to make sure everyone feels all right. Well, yes, in a sense they are. But true leaders are just as focused on the daily numbers, except they're also looking ahead with a long-term vision of where the company is going. The difference is that the leader fully realizes that the company's ultimate success begins and ends with the people.

Let me demonstrate this difference between a leader and a manager using four sticks. The first stick represents the leader. The second stick is the team, the third is processes, and the fourth is results. The manager type begins with the fourth stick, prioritizing the results and what he or she must do to bring them about. The leader, on the other hand, starts with himself or herself and then focuses on how the team is functioning. Leaders know that if they can get the first two sticks operating at a high level, they'll create the processes that will sustain the results. They also think about sustainability versus the success of the moment.

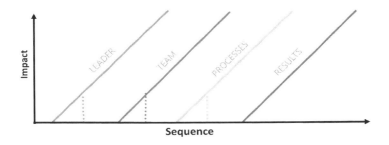

You can probably see why being a manager holds appeal. For me, it was an adrenaline rush. I was addicted to that month-end challenge. When I hit that number, it was time for the happy dance, to go out and get a couple of beers. But come Monday, I had to get my fix all over again.

Former first lady Rosalynn Carter once said, "A great leader takes people where they don't necessarily want to go, but ought to be." I agree that this statement summarizes, on its most basic level, what it means to *lead*. But from my perspective, what truly makes a leader is *how* he or she does it.

Early in my career, I helped businesses get to places they had not been before, but I was more of a manager than a leader. This meant progress came to a standstill when I left. I initially thought that proved how good a leader I was. Not the case. What it really meant was that I'd failed to grow my team (the second stick) well enough to continue our successes after I left.

If I had to pin down some common threads of true leadership, these are what I'd pick:

- People know you care.

- They believe that you know the path forward, not in great detail but in great direction.

- You are consistent in behavior and guidance.

- You model and stand for the values of the journey.

- You encourage others to live into their greatness, without caretaking.

- You meet them where they are and invite them to step forward.

- You communicate progress and acknowledge those responsible for achievements.

- You display grace when things don't go as planned.

- You are willing to sacrifice for the good of the team.

- You take care of yourself and continue to grow.

Although this Top Ten seems to be work related, you can see how these characteristics also apply at home!

Christine

Dad and I had a great exchange about leadership when he sent me this Quote of the Day a while back:

Good morning, Darling!

Here is your QoD! Enjoy!

Never underestimate your ability to be a leader, even if it only means being a good dad, mom, sibling, grandparent, or friend. You may only impact or lead a single person. However, we are all connected on this planet, and the seed you plant could travel far, with untold impacts to bloom and affect others.

—Ben Newman [11]

Ben Newman is a highly regarded performance coach, international speaker, and best-selling author.

I love this quote! It feels so true to me. When I was working, I loved to help people understand that leadership was not defined by the organization chart. It had nothing to do with position and everything to do with how I showed up. Time and time again, I was impacted by leaders on the shop floor who were at the "lowest level" of the org chart. For example, I had an operator say to me, "If you want to have the nicest house in the neighborhood, do you build it or tear all the others down?" Whoa! Through the analogy, he was expressing his opinion on the type of leaders our plant supervisors were, and he felt they were the latter. As you can tell, it impacted me, and I have shared that quote many times. That was almost twenty years ago!

I have also said to groups and individuals, "Never underestimate your impact." I believe that's the substance of this quote, and for you—I see many attributes of a leader in you. I know you are impacting others. Trust that you are, and cherish your gifts and responsibility!

I love you more than all the impact we can have when we choose!

Choosing Carmazzi

Having a connection like this with Dad meant I could get right to the heart of what I wanted to say about leadership and the impact we can have.

Hey, Dad! Happy Friday!

This is really good stuff. We've mentioned before that leadership doesn't come with a job title. It comes with how you present yourself and show up for those around you. I know when you and I started leadership training*, I would talk to my coworkers and friends about it. People wouldn't understand—they knew I didn't have any direct reports, so they were curious how I could lead. It invited more conversations than I was expecting! To me, it was obvious—the concept of personal leadership. However, our society has been formed to believe that leadership can only take place if you have people below you in a career setting. No way!

We all have an impact on the people we're around—think about all of the people you've impacted while riding the chairlift! Just by asking how their day was going, you've had a much larger impact than you might believe.

I know that the smallest of interactions with others can stay with me for a while. Granted, I hold on to things more than I should, but I am assuming that the owners of those interactions don't think twice about their words *and* aren't thinking that they would have a large impact on me!

> I love you more than all of the impact one small "hello" can have on others!
>
> *Christine is Being Friendly*

Note: About five or six years ago, Dad and I started a sort of book club, in which we read and discuss books focused on leadership, unpacking a chapter at a time.

Being a good leader means more than just having the right answers or having the guts to make an unpopular decision. Leading is a selfless act that requires leaders to remove their own feelings or wants from the equation. Leading is also about removing emotion from a decision and looking at facts versus feelings.

I'm still very much working on my leadership skills. If I had to evaluate myself on a martial arts-style belt-ranking system, I'd say I'm still at the white or yellow belt stage! It's challenging work taking emotion out of tense situations, but I'm also trying to stop assuming that other people's actions are personal. For example, if I'm working with a challenging colleague, I'm removing the self-talk that says, "Wow, this person must really not like me!" Instead, I'm transitioning to a solution-based thought process to help us achieve our goal.

Even if we take emotion out of the equation, it's important that people know we care. This is a major point for me because I have parents who have been obvious in their love for me. It's not as though I've had to fight for it. I want to emulate that kind of care.

I try to do this in various settings. For example, if I'm in a group and someone gets cut off mid-story, I'll try to bring the conversation back around to reengage that person's perspective or give an opening to resume the story. That may be a less obvious way of showing you care.

There's also the matter of consistency. All of my mentor figures have been super consistent. I've never had to worry about whether someone was going to show up to support me.

I don't have kids, but in my eyes, this is a great way not only to lead but to parent. My life would have turned out much differently if my parents hadn't modeled the kind of leading from the heart that I now want to emulate.

Tom

If I am leading from the heart, I am much more present. I'm hearing what is said and what is *not* said. I'm asking unassuming questions from a place of curiosity rather than manipulation. I'm inviting others to live to their capabilities and make their stand versus trying to "save" them. The vast majority of people do not need saving. As Therese used to say, "People are creative, resourceful, and whole."

When people ask me what course of action I think they should take, I'm slow to answer and quick to ask a question instead: "You're closer to the matter than I am. What do you think you should do?"

My goal is to be much more compassionate and empathetic, to put myself in other people's situations and be curious about their perspectives. It's a matter of being more selfless in all facets of my life, especially family. It is time to set my hourglass aside and find a way to be present with the person in front of me.

QUESTIONS FOR REFLECTION

What have you noticed when you lead from the heart? What does it feel like for you? What do you think it feels like for those you lead? What if you ask them?

I Love You More Than...

The Many Ways Love Is Revealed

Christine

What does love look like?

One way a dad can show love for his daughter is to comfort her after she thought she was going to be eaten by a bear. But I'm getting ahead of myself! Here's the story.

My favorite place on earth is McGregor Bay on the northern shore of Lake Huron, where my extended family has a cabin in the wilderness. Getting there is a trek, and once you're in, you're in one of the most remote regions around.

The summer before I graduated from college, I told my parents I wanted to spend six weeks at the cabin. Kind of a last hurrah before starting my big new career. Mom went with me, helping out as we drove to the marina, unloaded the car, loaded the small boat, and motored out to the cabin. There are a few nearby cabins but definitely not right up against each other. Usually, the neighbors and our family don't overlap our stays anyway.

This particular summer, a family friend named Jeff stayed at his cabin around the same time and looked out for us since Dad was busy with work and unable to come. We ran into him and his family. Everyone had a great time catching up.

One morning as we were leaving our cabin, Jeff shouted over, "Hey, just so you guys know, we had a bear at the cabin this morning."

Now, I had already styled myself the protector, since Mom is a petite woman and Dad wasn't around to fulfill that role. I waved back and said, "Okay, that's fine, thanks!" Mom and I went about our day, enjoying nature, and later that night, we grilled our food on a stone patio about fifteen feet from the house. It was a peaceful, relaxing evening.

Mom and I turned in for the night, sleeping in the same room at the back of the cabin. Around four or five in the morning, an air horn blasted out. I jumped awake. *Okay, well, that can't be good. It's close by. Definitely not way out in the bay. It's probably Jeff.* All I could think to do at that point was to wait it out. Falling back to sleep wasn't an option.

My mom slept right through it. I had to wake her up and explain what was going on. She squinted at me and said, "All right, let's see what happens."

I had a thought: there was a wireless speaker. I'd heard people play nonstop music on a loop to deter animals from coming on their property. So I cued up my playlist of country music, because for some reason I liked listening to country only in the summer. I cranked the volume up as far as it would go—which wasn't a lot—and left it playing. *That should do the trick.*

We tried to get back to sleep, but then we heard a massive *clang*, which got us both out of bed. We headed for the windows, and sure enough, there was a bear at our grill!

"Quick, here." Mom passed me an air horn.

Good idea. Dad had bought a bunch of new air horns at the beginning of the summer so we could be fully stocked for this kind of situation. I took it from her, but my hands were shaking. I was so scared. I was petrified. *This thing is somehow going to break into the cabin and eat me and Mom.*

Clearly, the music wasn't working. I aimed the air horn and squeezed.

Pffft.

Are you kidding me? It was just hissing. Absolutely no sound was coming out. It was brand new! By then I was shaking, but no matter how much I pressed, the horn just sputtered.

Maybe the music isn't loud enough. I started increasing it, but the speaker's volume control was locked. It wouldn't go any higher. The song playing was "Red Solo Cup" by Toby Keith, which isn't the loudest, rowdiest country song in the world, and it came out of the speaker so softly and quietly. It was just the faintest little sound, and I couldn't help thinking this was actually a nightmare.

Mom tried to figure out another air horn, and I was literally petrified. I couldn't yell. I could barely *speak*. "Just. Go. Away!"

I started clapping, and then Mom found a working air horn. Some combination of our racket finally made the bear walk away—walk, not run. The bear wasn't scared in the slightest. Maybe bothered a bit, but not scared.

I don't remember what we did the rest of that day, but we'd usually call Dad at night, or he'd call us, to catch up about the day. This time, Mom said, "Do not tell him there was a bear at the cabin."

But I couldn't hold it in. It was practically the first thing I blurted out: "Dad, we had a bear at the cabin!"

Talk about feeling love from far away. Dad went into full safety mode. He told me where there was a gun I could use to protect us and gave me helpful instructions over the phone. He didn't freak out or criticize, but he made sure he was there for me, even when he was several states away. There was no mistaking his love for me. My dad was my protector, regardless of distance.

Tom

I'd been worried about Christine's stay at the cabin because, at first, she wanted to go on her own. The place is accessible only by boat, and when you're there, you're relying on pretty basic technology.

But when Deb offered to go with her, I felt much better with them looking after each other. I tried to get up there as often as I could, but it really was them on their own. When Christine called about the bear, I chastised myself: "Well, that just figures! One of the times I'm not able to be there!"

She gave me the details rapid-fire of the malfunctioning air horn and the music being too quiet, and I could only wish that I'd been able to be there for the both of them. I couldn't imagine what that was like for Christine, our natural-born protector.

I walked her through how to use the gun I had in the cabin. It was a bit heftier than ones she'd used before, so she would have to take extra precautions if she were forced to fire it!

It was a situation with overlapping expressions of love. There was me, being away from my family and doing my best to provide long-distance comfort so I could help them process the challenge they had faced and prepare for a possible repeat encounter with the bear. But there was also Christine's urge to protect her mother against a scary unknown.

When I think of love, I divide it between illegitimate and legitimate. Illegitimate love expects love back in a conditional, transactional sense—I love you, so now you have to love me back. But legitimate love is loving someone regardless of what is received in return; it's unconditional.

My dad never talked about love. And yet, from kindergarten through high school, he missed hardly any of my baseball games. I was just an average player, not a standout. But Dad never suggested areas for improvement. He never critiqued. He just sat in the stands and cheered.

If he never spoke about love, how did I know he loved me legitimately? Because he was a workaholic, and I knew he was leaving work to come watch me. He went right back to work after the game. No matter how I played, his love for me never changed, and I knew he would show up at the next game. We never went together; he would just appear.

This had a major impact on my perception of love. I had friends who were very good at baseball—at least one guy was drafted by the Pittsburgh Pirates—but whose dads never showed up in the stands. For me, it was further confirmation of Dad's unspoken love.

Dad never said he loved me until the last two years of his life. He lived until he was ninety-two.

Fast forward to adulthood. I found myself unwilling to give love until it was received, and even then, I was skeptical. The birth of our children pushed me down the road to unconditional, legitimate love. I knew our children's love came with no conditions attached. They gave love because of who I was.

Part of my motivation for starting the Quotes of the Day went beyond wanting to offer Christine insights into leadership in a tumultuous time. Of course, that was what I wanted to get across, but the *why* was the desire to convey love in a multitude of ways. I also wanted to let Christine know through every quote just how much she meant to me. This was another way of providing sanctuary.

Not long ago, I sent Christine this one from a famed theologian:

Good morning, Darling!
Here is your QoD:

Love takes up where knowledge leaves off.
—Thomas Aquinas [12]

Thomas Aquinas was an Italian Dominican friar born in 1225. What I really dig about this quote is the exponential impact of love. For me, knowledge is somewhat linear, especially if it is intentional. Meaning, if I want to learn something, I focus on it, and it has the desired impact. Sometimes knowledge can be nonlinear when unplanned—like early in my career when I was in a meeting with the CEO and senior management and I "helped" a president of a business unit "see" that he really did not understand his customer. I thought I was so smart by helping everyone see. Well, guess what. What we think we know, we really don't. That is exactly what happened to me! I had no idea I was trashing this president in front of his boss and his boss's boss! And my brashness was reflecting poorly on me, much more than the strategic weaknesses of the president. This incident created a huge awareness for me.

Love is an accelerant in all environments where it is present. For me, when love enters a relationship, I am much more curious, much more present, much more energetic, and much more compassionate. All of that leads me to growth and development. It also leads to more influence and more impact.

There is an old adage: "People don't care what you know until they know you care."

I love you more than the power of love.

Loving Papa

Christine's response touched on Aquinas's quote from a different angle.

Hey, Daddio!

This is a unique twist on love—I hadn't thought of it in relation to knowledge. I think in order to be truly successful in all facets of life—career, family, friends, personal—you have to have a balance of both love and knowledge. Just one or the other won't get you over the finish line!

Gosh—what a learning opportunity you had early in your career. Luckily, you learned from that experience and transitioned to a more balanced state!

This quote made me think of parenting—you and Mom surely did not have all of the answers or expertise for how to raise two kids. When those concerns or questions came into play, that is where your love took over! And Mike and I turned out all right! Whew!

I love you more than all of the ways we can combine heart and head!

Christine Is Intellectual Yet Heartfelt

Tom (continued)

Loving your neighbor—or, in this case, your child—isn't the end, and it isn't the beginning. In a way, self-acceptance has to lead. How can you love others if you don't love yourself?

I used to beat myself up with a lot of negative self-talk. Usually, I'd critique myself in the shower at the start of the day as I reflected on the actions of the previous day and thought of my agenda for the current one. I thought it helped keep me sharp and open to improvement. I set the bar high, and I expected to reach it—no excuses!

I found plenty to beat myself up about, and when I was in the mode, the critique didn't stop with me. I tended to be very critical of others. I saw the glass as half empty. Some of that pessimism was fed by my work experience as a manufacturing operations guy. I was always looking for that gap, searching for ways to improve and remove waste. You're never done, though. There's no such thing as perfection. There's only the futile pursuit of it.

I found great help in the leadership classes I took, facilitated by Therese. She would ask me and the other participants what was important to us. We shared openly about treating others with respect and being helpful. But when she asked how we were showing respect and grace to ourselves, the room went quiet. The whole tenor changed. People, myself included, realized that we weren't giving ourselves any grace, respect, or love.

As time passed, I realized that negative internal dialogue was not only unhelpful; it was draining. More importantly, as my faith in God grew, I realized that I was passing judgment on one of God's creations, something I wasn't qualified to do. I had to shift my view of myself, so I altered the internal dialogue to questions like: "What did I learn? What am I going to do differently?"

This was a very important shift because I realized that it was going to be incredibly difficult to exercise true love toward my family and friends if I didn't even love myself.

Christine

We try to be as unselfish as possible so that we can better express love to others, but to some degree, self-acceptance has to be selfish. I believe that it starts with listening to our bodies and what feels good, because if we don't, we can shortchange the people we're trying to love.

I've been in situations where, even though my social and physical tanks felt empty, I still went out with my friends or said yes to social gatherings. Once I was out with people, I knew right away that I'd made a mistake. Maybe I wasn't giving my friends my full attention. Maybe I was outright yawning. Either way, my gut was correct: "You should have stayed home."

That's never how I want to be remembered or how I want to show up. So I give myself grace to turn down a social event every now and then, knowing that when I am fully recharged, I'm respecting myself and my loved ones.

The deeper I get into life, the more I realize that the relationships I have are really important to me. I don't feel like I need a bunch of acquaintances. I want thoughtful and genuine connections, so I expect my friends to reschedule if they're not feeling up to hanging out rather than push through out of social obligation. Because I know when I do that, I'm not showing my best self.

I share Dad's views about the need to quiet judgmental self-talk. If I shouldn't judge anyone else, then why am I putting so much judgment on myself? So, if I'm going to start respecting myself, what does that look like? In some cases, it means shying away from stretching myself too thin.

Forgiveness, too, plays a major role in how we treat ourselves and others. We can't have a meaningful relationship with someone if forgiveness isn't involved. It can certainly be hard at times. In difficult situations, I like to put myself in someone else's shoes. I also like to remember that, whatever my frustrations might be, I'm the cause of them. I always have a choice of how to react to instances that might not be favorable. Just because I'm in a bad mood doesn't mean that I have to take someone else down with me.

One winter, my husband and I hit an unexpected eighteen-hour travel day when we trekked to the East Coast. The last leg of the grueling trip was by rental car, two hours from Boston to New Hampshire. We got to the rental car company after midnight. When the attendant accidentally dropped my ID into a machine and struggled to get it out, another fifteen minutes was added to our already long day!

Instead of getting upset or showing my frustration, I pushed myself to laugh at the circumstances and was kindhearted toward the attendant. As easy as it would have been to jump to anger, I think choosing love and grace helped the entire interaction go as smoothly as possible. Besides, there was no point in making the attendant feel upset.

When turning that lens on the Quotes of the Day, I believe that forgiveness, along with trust, makes up the framework to have these kinds of conversations with my dad. Actions always speak louder than words, and knowing that I can express my thoughts and emotions without judgment is incredible. I also have security knowing that if I say something out of line, Dad will not only forgive me but continue to love me.

It might be easy to say the words *I forgive you*, but to feel truly accepted and loved after doing or saying something that feels unforgivable is incredibly rare, and it's something I always get from Dad.

Tom

Kindness, patience, curiosity, and grace are related. When I meet someone who is open, patient, gentle, and attentive, our relationship progresses quickly. Otherwise, I put up shields that slow the relationship.

I believe that kindness invites kindness. When I bring it, others bring it, even if the interaction or relationship is a little guarded at first. For example, I recently needed new summer tires for my car. I had already taken the old summer tires to the service center where I bought them, but I ended up ordering new tires from a different store that's within walking distance. I called the manager of the old service center to thank him for all he had done for us and to explain why I was switching to a competitor. I also offered to pay him to dispose of the old tires he was storing. I was literally reading the credit card number to him when he stopped me and said, "No charge. Thank you for being our customer. We'll take care of it." I believe he did that partially due to the kindness and respect I showed him.

Likewise, true forgiveness and unconditional love go together for me. In the same way that there is legitimate and illegitimate love, I believe that there is legitimate and illegitimate forgiveness. Legitimate forgiveness is when I forgive and expect nothing in return, either in the moment or later. There's no expectation that says, "You owe me."

Also, when I love people unconditionally, I am eager to forgive. I see them for who they are, warts and all—just like me—so I expect things to happen that require grace and forgiveness.

Most importantly, forgiveness requires reengaging. For example, I might respond to someone's apology like this: "Of course, I forgive you. I believe I know your heart. Now, let's go for a walk and catch up." Why such a jump from forgiveness to reengagement? I want to take responsibility for getting the relationship back on track. I shouldn't keep others in time-out, as though they have to earn their way back into the relationship. If that were the case, I wouldn't really have forgiven them. If I forgive, the slate should be wiped clean.

That used to be difficult for me to do because I considered the thing that happened in the moment to be a true indicator of who that person was. Forgiving, then, didn't mean moving on. It meant I was watching the person I had supposedly forgiven like a hawk, and he couldn't climb out of the hole because I was judging everything about him. It was an extrapolation of the negative self-talk I gave myself.

I had to lean hard on my faith. It was easy to tell myself that Christ loves all of us and He forgives us all, but then I'd add, "Except for me, because of all the things I have done, the people that I've laid off or fired. God isn't going to forget that. He has got other people who are much closer to the finish line of forgiveness than I am."

And that's just not true. That's not how God does forgiveness. My belief that I was a worse person than others I knew didn't somehow make it more difficult for God to welcome me into His arms. I had to accept His forgiveness if I was truly going to forgive others.

The following is a Quote of the Day that Christine and I shared in the context of forgiveness:

Good morning, Darling!

Here is your QoD:

Inner peace can be reached only when we practice forgiveness. Forgiveness is letting go of the past, and is therefore the means for correcting our misperceptions.

—*Gerald Jampolsky* [13]

Gerald Jampolsky, MD, author of *Forgiveness: The Greatest Healer of All*, was an internationally recognized authority in the fields of psychiatry, health, business, and education.

I believe Gerry is on to something. I know for me that forgiveness is a huge stress reliever and distraction remover. When I feel I have been wronged or disrespected, I get tense and I think about it a lot. Once I forgive, I am much calmer and can focus on those things that are more important. I believe the Serenity Prayer is a version of this.

People have said that you can forgive but never forget. I am not sure if I believe that completely. When I don't forget, I still tend to think about it, so I really have not moved on. I get the intention is to ensure we are not burned again. And if there are to be continued interactions of impact, I might agree. However, if not, I want to forget as well.

I love you more than all the millimeters between Chicago and Portland!

Forgiving and sometimes forgetting father

Good morning, Forgiving! You were up early this morning!

I agree with you! If I am living in a state of constant worry or concern about not forgiving someone, that absorbs all of my time and energy. It is the worst! And like you, I tend to take things like this very personally, when most of the time, I shouldn't! When I give too much energy to not forgiving someone, I'm giving the situation too much power. Like you said, the Serenity Prayer helps center me and bring me back to a reality that revolves around *my* happiness and things that I can control! What someone else does is not one of those things! This is a great reminder that forgiveness is always an option. It is trust that is harder to achieve in a relationship!

I love you more than all of the pizza in the world (had a delish pizza last night, yum!).

xoxox!

Reminders Carmazzi

Tom (continued)

Our love shows up in many ways. My wife, Deb, is amazing at serving others. She conveys the words *I love you* by her actions. She'll put together care boxes for Christine and Mike on holidays. There's never any doubt about where her heart is.

I only hope I can continue to do the same as I reach out to Christine through our time spent together and our shared Quotes.

Christine

I turned twenty-seven not long ago. Cameron and I had birthday dinner plans for early in the day, at quarter of six. My brother, Mike, texted me an hour before and asked if he could stop by to wish me a happy birthday.

I texted back, "Sure, but before 5:30 because we're headed to dinner right after."

His response: "Okay, be there ASAP!"

There was a knock at our door at 5:20. There's Mike, out of breath, holding a plate of cookies! He had baked them, frosted them, and ran the couple of blocks over to our apartment.

I knew I was truly loved, in a way more than words could express. It was like I was back in the family cabin and clutching the phone as Dad offered his words of comfort.

QUESTIONS FOR REFLECTION

What does love look like to you? How has your life been impacted by forgiveness or the lack thereof? What does your self-talk tend to sound like? As a result of this awareness, how will you love and forgive yourself and the people in your life differently?

Ego and Judgment:
The Basket Over Your Light

Tom

Early in my career, especially after I got my MBA, I was very quick to judge the business acumen of folks. And guess what—most of the time, I judged mine to be superior. Consequently, I didn't want to hear other people's perspectives. If they wanted to share their wisdom, I would be very determined to show them mine was greater, resulting in the conversation concluding prematurely.

Ego and judgment run the risk of derailing not just a conversation but a relationship. I see them as two separate yet connected things. Ego fuels judgment. Said differently, because of my ego, I will judge people. I will compare them to one another and declare simple thumbs-up or thumbs-down verdicts.

I used to judge a lot. Today, I'm leaving more and more of that to God because it's His job to judge, not mine. This also pertains to my tendency to judge myself as ruthlessly as I judge others, if not more so.

I want to differentiate between judgment and appraisal or assessment. As mentioned above, judgment contains a lot of ego for me. I am the judge of right or wrong. I usually don't test my assumptions, either. And the judgment is really about me, rather than the other person. However, it feels different when I am appraising or assessing, which feels less like taking a position and more like conveying a perspective. The person is fully at choice, and I am unattached to that choice. The act is to share wisdom, which for me is enough. I don't have to convince or win for the sake of my ego.

What role does curiosity play in this? If I'm not curious to have a dialogue instead of a one-way discussion, there's no relationship forming. For me, being curious means being truly present. I'm really listening to what you have to say versus thinking about my next question. That's just another form of ego-based control that lets me show how smart—or maybe not smart—I am.

There's still a danger of falling back on my ego when I'm asking questions and trying to be as curious as I can. I may not be truly curious, meaning that I ask a leading question, whether intentionally or not. I might ask, "What do you really like about your work? Is it the interactions with your clients? I know, for me, when I was doing your type of job, that's what I really liked."

You can see in those questions the lack of actual curiosity and the inability to let go of control. If I were really interested in you as a person, I'd ask, "Please tell me about yourself." There's a huge difference.

It comes down to the nature of my questioning. Am I asking in a nonleading, open-ended way? Is my true aim to hear your perspective without somehow trying to bias you?

Christine

I view ego and judgment as two separate things, but I agree with Dad that they're connected. For me, judgment is shaming or scoffing at someone's actions that you disagree with. I'm not saying that these actions can't be ones you perform yourself; however, in that specific moment of judgment, there is an added level of skepticism and shame placed on that individual.

Ego, on the other hand, is a blindfold to reality. It's active when I view myself as perfect, or nearly perfect, and it blinds me to what's actually going on. For example, ego usually occurs in settings that are larger than just myself, and there is a reduced level of unbiased, factual listening and learning.

There's a lack of humility in ego. I feel like I have no ability to see how I really am. I'm looking in the mirror through rose-colored glasses, but I'm the only person wearing them.

My husband and I recently headed back East to visit my family at our cabin in Canada. I tried to work while traveling, which is never a good idea. Cameron and I took a red-eye from Portland to Chicago. We ended up in the seats ahead of the exit row, which do not recline, and the headrests hit the backs of our heads in such a way that our chins stayed pointed down, no matter how we rearranged.

Let's just say that neither of us slept on the flight. We landed in Chicago and boarded our plane to Toronto, which had a sudden fuel gauge issue. We deplaned.

Our pilot found another plane, so that was great—until we got delayed again because the second plane was having problems with, of all things, the lavatories. The double malfunctions caused us to miss our connection out of Toronto to Sudbury, where we needed to arrive roughly four hours before sundown to make it safely to the cabin.

At this point, we'd been traveling for fourteen hours. We were both tired and grumpy, but neither of us wanted to give up. So we rode a taxi two and a half hours north to meet my parents halfway to Sudbury.

I had been trying to work this whole time, desperately connecting to airport and aircraft Wi-Fi, as well as whatever hotspots I could find. Throughout the day, a recurring problem had come up: our company had pallets of damaged packaging sitting in a warehouse. This issue had been going on for quite some time, and the blame continued to get kicked around. The vendor claimed it was the warehouse's fault and vice versa. In previous instances, when I would try to address the issue with either party, they would get defensive or "ghost" my emails. I was making zero progress.

I'd had enough. I lit into the vendor in an email, unleashing my frustration and exhaustion on them, blaming them for the poor quality of pallets and palletization and demanding refunds for the hundreds of thousands of dollars we'd spent on packaging we couldn't use.

That email was a bad idea. My words came across much harsher over a screen than I had intended. Neither my boss nor the vendor appreciated my lashing out. It turned out that there was a combination of reasons the boxes were unusable, and unfortunately, given the nature of the issue, we couldn't get much money back. The only thing we could do was put measures in place for future shipments to ensure that these issues didn't persist.

I've since recovered the relationship with the vendor, but I still feel guilty for how I let my ego take over. Things would have turned out much better if I'd set aside *me* and focused on the problem at hand, working with people to find solutions instead of dumping my frustrations on them. But in the moment, those frustrations were the biggest problem, according to my mind.

It's not easy. I've always considered myself horrible at hiding my emotions. Lots of people have told me that I'm an open book. Even if I think I'm withholding judgment, it often doesn't look that way to my peers. I rarely speak my judgments about others, choosing instead to keep them in my head, but that doesn't make it better. I'm improving my recognition of my internal judgments and putting a stop to them before they burst out like they did in that terrible email.

Tom

Later in my career, my boss transferred me from the corporate office to operations, which I saw as a win since that's where I wanted to be. My new boss had me shadow him for a few months. During meetings, I would run the show while he quietly observed.

After one of our meetings, he asked me, "Tom, have you thought about going into a meeting without an agenda?"

"What? Why would you even call a meeting if you didn't have an agenda?" I thought he was crazy.

He replied, "Consider walking in there without handing out a piece of paper with the agenda on it."

"Okay, sure. I'll think about that." As soon as he walked away, I thought to myself, "He has no idea what he's doing. I think he's lost it!"

When I finally tried following his suggestion, I held a meeting without handing out a paper agenda. Afterward, I asked my boss, "Well, what did you think?"

He gave me a sly smirk and said, "Tom, everyone in that room knew you had an agenda, whether it was written down or not."

I had gone for the letter of the law but not the heart. My ego was still clouding my interactions with others. I assumed that I always had to be right, and my rules weren't to be questioned or broken.

It took me a couple of years to see what he wanted me to see: that by systematically reviewing points I wanted to cover, I was stifling the curiosity and creativity. He was hoping I would go in armed with just a topic to discuss and open the room up for dialogue and brainstorming. His goal was for me to hold meetings in which the conversation could flow and I could truly utilize the gifts and talents of my colleagues.

It's no surprise that this behavior also showed up at home. Mike had a curfew when he was a teenager, and he was remarkable about almost always being *precisely* on time. It's almost like he hung out in the garage or synchronized his watch to mine!

If he was ever late, I didn't ask why. He'd broken the rules. I just quickly and curtly told him, "Your curfew tomorrow night will be thirty minutes earlier, and those reductions will continue until you can't go out anymore."

There's no grace there at all, only my ego insisting that I was right and my judgment assuming that he was willfully breaking my rules. Fortunately, as I matured, I would ask why he was late and, as a result, almost always learned more about his life and who he was.

One of Mike's other strengths is that he will give an honest answer to a genuinely asked question, even if, as a parent, your first instinct is, "I'm not sure I want to know." So I learned to engage him calmly and curiously, believing that he fully intended to be home on time and assuming that, if he wasn't, something unexpected must have happened.

This helped improve the trust in our relationship. One evening when he was late, Mike related that his friend's car had broken down in a rough neighborhood and the kids were scrambling to get it going again. Despite his intention to hit the curfew target and keep his promise, he got home just a couple of minutes late.

Now, if I'd hammered him, things would have gotten ugly. Our relationship would have taken a hit because I would have failed to see or appreciate all his best efforts. Since I believed in Mike's heart, I was curious about what had happened and believed his every word.

Age has been very humbling for me. I've been shown time and time again that I'm not the smartest or most capable person in the room. I can truly learn from everybody. Having said that, I believe that I have been put here for a reason, and I am to participate as impactfully as I can from a place of wisdom and compassion.

What does that look like? It looks like truly hearing what Christine has to say when I send her a Quote of the Day. It means letting the dialogue at a dinner party wander where it will, listening intently and learning what others have to say. It means unbridling the dialogue versus controlling it.

I would love for my humility to grow every day, every week, every month. It's up to me to teach myself to be more inquisitive and less directive.

Christine

Conversations are not just one person chatting while someone else listens. They're a constant back and forth. To make sure a conversation is successful, I have to approach it like a learning experience. Even if I have a piece of advice or helpful information for the other person, it's rare these days for me simply to offer it up. Instead, I'll wait for when, or even if, there's a right time in the conversation, whereas before I might have bulldozed it in where it didn't belong.

I had a rough time with my judgmental response when I was traveling all day, so I think it's fitting to revisit this next Quote of the Day now because of where Dad was when he wrote it. It was once said of Eleanor Roosevelt, "It is better to light a candle than to curse the darkness,"[14] and here's what Dad relayed to me from the Louisville airport:

> Whoa, Ellie strikes again!
>
> What I love about this quote is the suggestion to get out of victimhood and address the issue. *And* sometimes addressing the issue is quite simple.
>
> I know there are times that I can choose victimhood, and it's usually under stress or when I am tired. During those times, it is small stuff, like someone sitting too close to me at the airport this morning. There was plenty of space; all I had to do was move. I did, and suddenly I felt better and stopped my mind from complaining. Amazing!
>
> And I was able to do my QoD! Life is good!
>
> I love you more than all the ways to get off the Victim-Villain-Hero triangle for the betterment of me and others!
>
> *Light-seeker Carmazzi*

Taking action to rein in our egos and refrain from judging others is a must, or else our old habits will take back control all over again. This is how I responded to Dad:

> *Wow!* You were up awfully early! I hope you had a nice but quick trip to Louisville!
>
> Oh gosh, this is so cool. The simplicity of addressing the issue versus letting it fester is so key to moving on and continuing about your day! I love the example you shared about this morning. You could have easily stayed seated and just fumed over why they would choose to sit so close to you, *or*, like you did, you could take action, remove yourself, and calm down.
>
> For me, I notice that to get to a place of awareness and reconciliation, I need to remove myself and take a walk, or get some form of exercise. I usually calm myself down or think of ways to handle what's coming next. I've noticed it is nearly impossible to start problem solving when I'm in the same physical space. Interesting stuff!
>
> I love you more than all of the ways we can take a step back, become aware, and move on!
>
> *Christine's Getting Outside*

Christine (continued)

It's always worth taking that step back after a conversation, or even in the moment, to see if we're really paying attention to what the other person has to say; otherwise, we're not making the connections we truly hope for. As humans, we tend to judge quickly. All we see in a given situation is our own perspective. We puff ourselves up, and if we're not careful, we can bring our own judgments into the situation without taking a moment to listen and understand. When we take the time to listen, we can have more productive conversations and relationships that produce real results. Instead of steamrolling over others' opinions, we can collaborate and work toward greater solutions.

QUESTIONS FOR REFLECTION

Considering that "it is better to light a candle than to curse the darkness," how have you let your light shine recently? On a scale of 1 to 10 (with 10 being *always*), how often do people see your light? How would your life be different if you increased that number? What can you do to raise that number?

I Love You More Than...

Living Out the Values
We Hold Dear

Tom

I played a lot of golf between the ages of twelve and six-teen. You could find me out on the links pretty much every day. I was nearly always alone.

This was when I was grappling with my stuttering, trying to work through it, but also withdrawing from those around me who would mock my speech. It's no surprise why I fell in love with the game. It was so much fun, and I wouldn't have to play against anyone—or speak to anyone, either. It was just me against the course.

It occurred to me at some point that it would've been really easy to cheat. Nothing was stopping me from rolling the ball out of the rough or laying down another ball or taking an extra shot. No one was around. No one was watching.

That's not to say my game didn't need any help. A lot of rounds turned pretty ugly, and I could have improved my score drastically by dropping the ball just a foot away from where it had landed.

For whatever reason, cheating just didn't feel right. Something inside of me said, "No, you're not going to do that. You hit it where it landed." To this day, I don't know what prompted me to take the high road, but I've always thought of golf as a good sport for building the fundamentals of honesty and integrity.

This scenario comes back to me when I start thinking about the values I hold dear. You'll hear lots of people mention their values, the supposedly nonnegotiable virtues by which they conduct their lives, but what does that mean? What are their actual values?

Most people, when you ask them directly, can't put what they believe into words. I serve on the board of the business school at a university and was offered the opportunity to mentor their MBA students, which I happily accepted. Each quarter, I sit down individually with anywhere from one to five students who are eager to talk about where they are in life and what they want to achieve.

My first question is always: "What do you want out of this relationship?" They usually have lots of questions about how they can strengthen their business acumen or how they can become a vice president of sales or even a CEO. I nod and tell them, "That's great. That's good stuff. But we're going to start at a different place."

I'm not sure what they're expecting me to say next, but the words they hear are: "What are your values?"

That really catches them off guard. Can you imagine how you'd react if you were at a social gathering and this question came up? "Hey, nice to meet you. Tell me about your values." It's not exactly surface chatter.

But that's the point. I want them to really think about the things that are important to them and, even better, how they can articulate those things. Why would I bug them about this? My fundamental belief is that possessing this inner compass is essential. Our values can and should be our foundation, our bedrock, our North Star. Without them, I know I could be influenced by what seems to make the most sense in the moment versus a grander scheme or greater calling. It's not until we establish this foundation that our true life goals can be both achieved and sustained.

Defining values isn't as easy as you might think. It is rare that a student has been able to state his or her values and, more importantly, what those values mean. Usually, the student goes quiet and says something like, "No one has ever asked me that before." Or "I'm not sure. I've never thought about it."

In defining their values, I want the students to get to the heart of the matter versus what they might find on Dictionary.com. Then I ask them to spend the next two weeks observing how their values did or did not show up, and they must be prepared to share stories of what they learned. This usually takes three or four sessions to nail down.

It's not easy! For example, I can ask them, "What does integrity mean for you?" You'd think it would be easy to define *integrity*, but I've seen evidence that saying the word is far easier than living it out. When I was working in manufacturing, the supervisor had visual boards on the shop floor to show how production was going. A red dot meant that you didn't hit the quantity goal for the hour. The supervisor would write a question on the board: "What caused you to get a red dot?" Employees were then invited to write comments on the board in response, so everyone could get to the root of the issue.

I thought it was great—except, the supervisor would not respond. To my mind, there was an implied contract that if you asked the question and got a response, then you should acknowledge the reply. When you don't, you're out of integrity.

Later I conducted leadership classes for supervisors. I'd look around the room and ask, "Who in here does not have integrity? Raise your hand." Of course, no hands went up. Then I'd hold up pictures of those visuals on the shop floor, which showed, in essence, these implied promises being broken. "Whose visuals are these?"

Someone would reply, "Those are mine."

"Okay, someone answered your question and told you why they got a red dot. There's no reply from you. So, tell me, how does your integrity show up in this situation?"

The room would go dead quiet.

It's just a simple word everyone uses or throws around. Probably half the corporate mission, vision, and values statements in North America contain the word *integrity*. But what does it really mean? How does it show up?

We all have to ask ourselves that question at some point.

Christine

We've seen just how important my parents took their job of instilling values in me and my brother when we were growing up—hence the Carmazzi Rules posted on the refrigerator! Humbleness, honesty, leadership, and integrity were key traits we were supposed to learn and demonstrate.

Humbleness was a tricky one that showed up frequently early in my life while I was playing sports. I could be pretty sassy on and off the playing field, which left my parents the task of keeping my ego in check and helping me mellow over time. With honesty, I often was caught in little fibs early in my life, and I would receive appropriate punishment for those until I learned to be honest.

My mom's been a wonderful example of leadership. When I joined Girl Scouts, she signed up as a leader and took the task so seriously that she stayed involved for several years after I was done. She was a great cheerleader and mentor, encouraging me to stick with the Scouts in middle school, when I thought it had outlived its usefulness and my interest had waned. But Mom gently steered me, saying, "You should probably continue on. There's a lot there to offer."

I didn't realize what she meant until I was able to take the individual service trips that Girl Scouts offered throughout the summer to twelve different locations ranging from Iceland to the Amazon, from Europe to Fiji. The process for applying was intense. It was almost like filling out college application paperwork!

Each of these trips had a specific focus. At one point, I was fascinated by marine biology and thought about pursuing it as a career, so I applied for trips that offered me ecology-based and conservation options.

It was more than just work and studies. It gave me the opportunity to see the world on my own, visiting places I'd never been to. So, in a way, it was my mom's leadership that helped me take the risks to grow into my own leadership roles.

These values have guided my decisions tremendously, the most recent of which having to do with leaving my previous job. Without getting into too much detail, I was paired with a person who brought out some ugly sides of me and who went against not only the company values but also my own on a regular basis. When I'd had enough, I made a stand for what I believed by reporting to management what was going on.

Unfortunately, nothing changed. I knew I couldn't stick around and go against the principles I was raised with. There were certain things I wasn't willing to compromise, so I had to leave that job and find another one.

Dad and I had a great exchange about the ways our values mark us and how, just like I'd discovered, pursuing them can come with a cost. He sent me this Quote of the Day:

> Good morning, Darling!
> It is that hump day of Wednesday. And to get you over that hump, here is your QoD:

Sow a thought, reap an action; sow an action, reap a habit; sow a habit, reap a character; sow a character, reap a destiny.

—*Stephen Covey* [15]

Steven Covey is an acclaimed writer on leadership. He wrote *The 7 Habits of Highly Successful People*, which became a classic on leadership.

What I love about this quote is the linear nature of destiny and how all these things are connected. For me, there are two key points from this quote. It starts with our thoughts. So, how do I ensure my thoughts are pure and the catalyst to a destiny I want? I believe it starts with my values and how deeply ingrained they are. The deeper they are, the more they drive my thoughts. In essence, my thoughts become the conduit for putting my values into action. My values become the limiter or governor of my thoughts. They reduce the deviation to the "dark side."

Interestingly, I just further clarified my values and aligned them with those I helped create at the company where I retired. I felt they needed a refresher to further focus my thoughts. It's no accident that I start with values when coaching executives and people with MBAs. We identify them, define them, and then see how they come to life every day, or not.

The second point is that this is like a chain that can break at the weak link, at any time. And that disconnect will dilute my destiny. Said differently, I can only reap what I sow. Sow nothing, reap nothing; sow weeds, reap weeds; sow roses, reap roses.

Destiny is very intentional to me. I cannot create a destiny through luck. I have to put in the work. Good news: I love my job!

I love you more than all the cool things in life that start with a dose of discipline!

Chain Link Carmazzi

Dad's email forced me to put some of my life's turbulence into greater perspective.

Hey, Pops,

This quote screams, "Nothing good in life is free." Thinking about Cam's and my marriage and this point in our lives, it could be very easy for me to show negative emotions towards our move or be upset that he's on vacation or taking time away from being together. Yet, I know that is not how we maintain a healthy relationship! I couldn't just act selfishly and expect to get selflessness in return.

I like your last point about destiny being a chain—if you allow certain aspects of your life to fail, the path to destiny can become much less clear or attainable. What you put in, you get out!

I love you more than all the ways we can strengthen our chains to better ourselves!

Christine Is Focusing on Cohesiveness

Tom

During my college years, I was a co-op student at a big accounting firm, working out of their Dayton office. During one meeting, folks from the Cincinnati office were bashing the Dayton office, just slandering them left and right. I sat there and didn't say anything because my brain was shouting, *This isn't right!* Yet, by virtue of being there, I got in trouble with the managing partner of the Dayton office because I had been present for what was, in effect, harmful gossiping.

My managing partner was right to be upset with me. I should have spoken up in defense of the people I was working with. Instead, my silence condoned the behavior of their attackers. He expected me not only to know my values but to stand for them!

My values seem very solid until I feel that I've been disrespected; then grace, gratitude, and love can go out the window, unfortunately. I tend to turn to fight-or-flight behavior. And guess what—many times, the person I was offended by had no intention of disrespecting me. I had judged (there is that word again!) that person's actions to be disrespectful and had taken them personally. I failed to be curious and test my assumed reality.

My values haven't been static. When I was younger, I was focused on getting things done and keeping my commitments—back to that emphasis on numbers instead of people. But as I matured and realized that I needed to focus more on other people, I shifted my values. Grace, love, and gratitude took their place at the top of the list instead of at the bottom.

Recovery became key. If I steered from my values in the midst of a dialogue, I wanted to recover my true north as quickly as possible. Early on, a day or two could pass before I realized, "Wow, I really screwed that up. I didn't show any grace or gratitude or love in the slightest!"

I set myself a different goal, one dictated by tennis, which I was playing a lot of at the time. Between shots, you have just a few seconds to get back to the baseline and prepare to hit the next shot. That became my recovery goal. Even if I metaphorically chunked one into the net by making some thoughtless comment, I had mere seconds to get back to where I needed to be.

What did that look like from a practical standpoint? Sometimes I would call people back into a meeting to apologize, adding, "That's not something I want anyone to emulate."

Recently, I sent Christine a quote that had a profound impact on me because of what it teaches about our values: that, simply put, they're not just for show.

> Good morning, Christine!
> Here is your QoD:
>
> *Principles have no real force except when one is well fed.*
>
> —*Mark Twain* [16]
>
> Mark nailed this one! What I love about this quote is the importance of using or practically applying our principles or values. If only stated and never used, they really are not guiding me. They are simply a conversation piece versus a compass. I have had many opportunities to breach my values. And I wish I could say I never did. What I can say is that when I did, regardless of the rationalization used in the moment, I did not feel stable. I felt less tethered, rudderless.
>
> Very recently, I was in dialogue with someone who was going through some very challenging and emotional situations—things that could invite victimhood or anger to be the response. We talked for two and a half hours, and we kept coming back to the same place: "What do your values suggest is the best path forward? Not the other person's values, but your values." Guess what! This brought comfort, cohesion, and conclusion to the best path forward.

I love you more than all the ways our values help us/me stay to what is true north.

Values-aligned Papa

In her reply, Christine articulated her understanding of how vital it is for us not just to declare our values but to demonstrate them in a way that lets other people see that they're more than just words—they're a way of life.

Hey, Pops,

Wow—thank you for sharing your story about your recent lengthy but productive conversation with your friend. It sounds like you were able to remove the emotion for the other person and just focus on consistency and staying true to yourself.

We've talked a lot recently about the importance of living up to our values. I think Mark nailed it with this one. The only way our principles and values can be alive is if we practice them and honor them every day. I'm realizing, as I get older, this is easier said than done! It takes work and isn't easy, but it is fulfilling.

I love you more than all of the opportunities to be true to ourselves!

Christine is Focusing on Consistency!

QUESTIONS FOR REFLECTION

What are your values? On a scale of 1 to 10 (with 10 meaning that you are truly living them out every day and they are an integral part of your decision-making), how does your life reflect your values? How would your life be different if you were to focus solely on increasing that number? What can you learn from the specific ways you live out your values?

The Seduction of Busyness and Its Impact on Our Lives

Christine

Everybody seems busy all the time these days. I know there's nothing new under the sun, but it just feels like we've filled up our hours with more and more stuff to do. It's especially bad if you're hooked up to your phone throughout the day—the "distraction device," as I call it.

Not long ago, I decided to get off social media. Two months later, I could feel the relief of not needing to know everything that was going on at all times, but then I got an email from Instagram. The automated message politely informed me that I'd been banned from their platform, followed by helpful hints on how to get my account back.

This has to be spam. That was my first reaction. After careful investigation, however, I found that it really was Instagram. That was puzzling. Maybe I'd been hacked.

"Hey, Cameron," I asked my husband, "you're on Instagram. Can you go look at what my account is doing? You know, just search my username?"

"Sure." He punched in the information on his phone, then turned the screen to me.

Sure enough, there I was, but with zero posts, zero followers, zero anything. My account page existed, but Instagram had completely wiped out everything else. I shrugged and went through the process to prove I was me, which was funny when you think about it. I knew who I was, yet I was the one who had to prove my existence to the social media platform that had accidentally deleted my online life.

About four days later, I got a confirmation email saying that my account was up and running again, along with an apology for any inconvenience. That's when it struck me: in those four days, I didn't think twice about the loss of my account. My life hadn't changed at all.

Then I asked myself how I would have felt if the ban had come a few months earlier, before I'd made the decision to unplug from social media. There's no way to sugarcoat my reaction—I would have freaked out. I'd have been panicking for those four days. *Oh, no! I can't get on Instagram. I'll have to make a new account, or I'll have to repost everything! What am I going to do?*

Yet, there I was, feeling completely unimpacted. What it came down to was whether social media was benefiting me or if it was just keeping me from paying attention in real life. The answer was simple enough. As much time and effort as I was putting into maintaining an online presence, social media was not reciprocating that benefit back to me. So I had to kick the habit and stay off, no matter how the platform tried to entice me to return.

I found that social media provided me an excuse not to check in on friends and loved ones. It thwarted my attempts to maintain my awareness of the people around me and the aspects of their lives that are important to them. Of course, I could already see what they were up to by reading their profiles, but in an odd way, that depersonalized our connection. Why would I bother to reach out to them directly if I could swing by their Facebook pages, skim the latest happenings for a week, then go on with my life? The platforms intended to keep us connected encouraged only the thinnest, most impersonal of connections.

I think the truth of the matter is that, for me, social media was the greatest—and by that I mean the worst!—distraction from everyday life and the personal connections I wanted to maintain. I'd run to my phone when I was procrastinating, hence the fun name "distraction device." And then there's sleep, which might seem surprising, but I'm the kind of person who's very protective of my minimum eight hours every night. I can easily take a few more hours as an excuse to avoid the things I should be doing. I'll often make plans the night before to get some morning work done or maybe go to the gym, and it's easily about half of the time I'll ditch those plans to get more sleep.

That's not to say that more rest is a bad thing! Not at all. But you can see how even the most well-intended things in our lives can distract us from our goals. For me, it's due to the fear of being bored. I see "doing something" as productive, even if I'm becoming drained because of it. The closest I've come to getting away from busyness is being on a beach vacation. Just sitting on the sand and watching the waves helps me recharge.

I have heard of a few studies that suggest boredom is actually extremely helpful for brain power and function, but I still avoid it at all costs! Let's put it this way: I'm afraid of what I would do if I didn't have multiple things filling up my day! But the reality is that not doing anything at all can be productive.

Being too busy is perhaps one of the worst things we can do when we're trying to maintain the relationships we care about the most, especially when we're in the midst of an intimate conversation, but busyness is also a difficult thing to step away from.

Tom

I call it the seduction of busyness, which for me has two major aspects. Recently, it's popped up with regards to my faith, in which the temptation to keep busy steers me off the path of Christ, often without my even knowing it. There's no doubt that busyness has been part of my life for quite some time. Even back during my working days, when I wasn't as deep into my faith, it was easy to find things to do that might not have been particularly impactful.

The classic example would be our company's annual goals for personal development, which we set to ensure that we improved both individually and as a leadership team. As December 15 rolled around, the end of the year close at hand, we'd have pushed off our own development because we made ourselves busy with something else that, by comparison, wasn't as important. We'd rationalized that whatever else needed to be done was of greater value. To make a point of errant procrastination, my coach used to break down the word *rationalize* as *rational lies*, because we tend to tell ourselves lies like, "I have to get this done," instead of focusing on what's really important.

For many years, I felt that I had to *earn* my way. I could not be given anything. I'm not sure where or when that attitude originated, but I know it was definitely part of my career mindset. I had to be busy, or I was not earning it—whatever "it" was. Being busy was some form of proof that I was making progress and that I was deserving of whatever I got. If I did nothing, well obviously, I would get nothing.

To call it an addiction might seem harsh, but it's really the best way to categorize what I experience. I am, therefore, an easy target for the seduction of busyness. I choose the word *seduction* because, as I grow in my faith journey, I realize that the devil loves for us to be busy. He does not have to get me to sin; he just has to keep me busy doing things that are not the most impactful for God's kingdom.

It really came to a head when I retired at the end of 2019, just ahead of the pandemic, but of course, I didn't know that was on the horizon. I'd given two years' notice, so there was time to shift my busyness from sixty hours a week down to forty or fewer, but when I stepped out of work for the last time, the emptiness in my daily routine was jarring.

Fortunately, my goal of skiing every North American location covered by the Ikon Pass helped because it provided me with a couple of months of busyness. But when I returned home in late March of 2020, I struggled to establish a new routine. I knew what I didn't want to do: play a lot of golf and tennis or watch TV all the time. But I was less certain of what I did want. I started walking with Deb and took a few road trips to Ohio to see Mom, but it wasn't until 2021 that things really solidified.

That's when I started mentoring MBA students and working with companies to breathe Christ into their organizations. Neither of those things was about money. They were about lending my time to efforts I thought were beneficial for others. My busyness was shifting to things of greater importance.

Christine

I think it's rather obvious and refreshing when people listen intentionally. Rather than change the subject or cut the conversation short, they ask thoughtful questions that often push the conversation deeper. Eye contact and body language set the stage in a big way, too.

It's important to stay aware during a conversation for the sake of relationship building. Without listening to what is being said to us, we're unable to form a deeper bond, to relate to one another, and to carry on a conversation. When I find myself distracted, my brain starts thinking about the next task at hand or about whatever is causing me stress. Those things crowd out what's being shared by the person I'm speaking with.

Ironically, I've also checked out of a conversation in an attempt to contribute better to that very conversion. I'm pretty sure lots of people do the same thing. Let's say someone mentions a topic I happen to know a little bit about. My mind starts racing around for ways I can contribute to the conversation on the same subject. I'll bet people notice when I've zoned out for that reason!

When Cameron and I were first dating, I was living in Arizona, and he was in Oregon. I would often visit him and his family for extended periods. During one trip, we went to a house party with some of Cam's high school friends. I didn't know anyone there besides him, but I tried to put myself out there and make friends, which had never been a strength of mine during school.

I started a conversation with a guy who was into photography. There we go—I'd found a shared interest. Being a college student at the time, I figured that other people at this party were in the same boat, or at least that's what my internal dialogue was telling me. Once the photography talk trailed, I leapt for the next topic. "So, where are you going to school?"

"I'm not in school." He gave me a funny look. "I didn't go to undergrad."

My mind went blank. I can't imagine what my face looked like. I had no clue what to say to him from that point on. My bias of coming from a high school with a very high graduation rate and an equally high rate of four-year undergraduate attendance set me up for failure. Instead of actually listening and providing thoughtful conversation, I derailed myself by fixating on what to talk about next.

One of the exchanges Dad and I had about a Quote of the Day comes to mind:

Good morning, Darling!

Here is your QoD!

The bad news is time flies. The good news is you're the pilot.

—Michael Altshuler

Michael Altshuler is a former business owner who became a motivational speaker, peak performance coach, and sales consultant. Altshuler is known for the book *Get Hired!: Land Your Dream Job*.

What I love about this quote is the recognition of how busy we all are, AND it is by our own CHOOSING. No Victimhood! We are as busy as we allow ourselves to be. For me, the busyness is about being clear with my yes's and no's. AND it is easier for me to say yes than it is to say no. Part of my challenge is I want to be liked and seen as helpful. The other part is I am not clear on how to choose between yes and no.

Recently, I have gained clarity on what is important and choosing things that align with my values and my purpose. I put those "big rocks" in the beaker first. That does help greatly. And yet it is still not easy! Even with that clarity, I still get trapped by the moment—the small stuff, or sand—and lose sight of longevity and legacy. That is my next level of improvement!

126

I love you more than all the opportunities to stay focused on the "big rocks" and not allow the "sand" of the moment to consume the space in my beaker.

Rocky Carmazzi

Hi, Dad!

Wow! I really like this quote—all for taking ownership of your own life, your decisions, and doing the most with it! At 26, I sure do know that time flies—I can't imagine how you must feel at 66! (Not a dig on age, just pointing out that you've had many more experiences throughout your life, and I bet they don't seem too far away!)

I think you're spot on. Sure, it's great to fill the time that we do have and to choose to do what WE want. But are we choosing to fill our time because we're bored or we think it's the "right" thing to do, or are we filling our time with positive actions that will better ourselves and those around us? Worth thinking about!

Regarding your challenge of deciding between yes or no, I think that's natural! Unfortunately, with some decisions, you won't know the right answer until you've decided. BUT as more opportunities are thrown your way, the more similarities will arise between situations, where you can make a more educated decision.

My current challenge is staying present—and not allowing time to fly while I think and wish about the future. That's a real struggle of mine. I don't want to look back on these days and wish I did more, or did things differently. Even though I know there's no good use in thinking about those things I cannot control, my mind often slips back to that old habit.

I love you more than all of the control we have to make our lives amazing!

Christine's Crafting Her Life

Christine (continued)

There's always time to learn and correct, especially when it comes to participating in important conversations. It may be easy to condemn ourselves when we consider how easily we get distracted from the important conversations in our lives. We easily pick up our phones when sitting across the table from our important people, and in reflecting on this behavior, we can be tempted to feel disappointed in ourselves. Instead, today is an opportunity to course correct and find our way back to healthy and undistracted connection with the ones we love.

QUESTIONS FOR REFLECTION

How do you stay focused on what's important? What can you do to make your distractions fewer and shorter? What would become possible in your life if you were to do so?

Getting Past Our Hard Outer Shell to Reach the Heart

Tom

It's probably the most common question that comes up in conversation when we first meet someone, after the introductory handshakes. It comes somewhere between "Where are you from?" and "How are you doing?"

"So, what do you do for a living?"

Several years ago, Deb and I invited Christine's soccer teammates and their families over to our place for coffee and donuts after one of their games—nothing fancy. Everyone was chatting in our living room and dining room, getting to know each other, as social adults are apt to do. One of the moms started going around the room, asking folks what they did for a living. I tried to steer clear, but there was no escaping what I considered to be perhaps the most irritating thing I could be asked in a conversation.

Eventually, it was my turn. "So, Tom, what do you do for a living?"

"I'm a dairy farmer."

"Oh." She looked puzzled. "Really?"

"Absolutely. I've got 120 cows on some land about twenty-five miles away. We milk them twice daily."

"How about that?" She still seemed baffled but continued on her way, conducting her employment census.

Not five minutes later, Deb came through the room, offering more coffee to the group. She had a bottle of cream from Jewel, our local market. The mom who'd been so insistent on finding out what everyone did for work spotted Deb and called out, "Wait, you don't use your own cream? You use store-bought cream?"

The odd comment might have confused other wives, but not Deb. She immediately locked onto me with an unamused gaze. This wasn't the first time I'd pulled a stunt like that. The mom looked at me. "What's going on?"

I fessed up. "I'm a COO of a manufacturing company."

She commented back, loud enough so everyone could hear, "Finally, someone who makes something!"

Her response illustrates the reason I don't like being asked or even asking, "What do you do for a living?" The answer immediately introduces a bias into the relationship. People have preconceived notions about every occupation under the sun, and the second you tell others what yours is, they try to fit you to those notions.

The question has irritated me since very early in my career. I'm not sure when my irritation arose, but it was likely sometime after I became a CPA. Most of my socialization at that time involved other accountants, so the job question rarely came up. It was only after my career accelerated and shifted that I began to feel the pressure.

Some of it has to do with my upbringing. My family had humble roots, which made me suspicious of folks who bragged about what they had done. I knew I didn't want to be one of those people, believing humility to be the better trait. Accordingly, I tend to downplay what I've achieved as not really being as important as who I am. Success is a by-product, not a definition.

I also tend to downplay my achievements when it comes to sports. When people ask me if I play golf, I say, "I play a little"—which is true, though as a teenager, I played twenty-seven to thirty-six holes every day. As a result, I became really good, and that skill carried over into adulthood, to the point that I can play well without practicing. Sometimes after a round of golf, my playing partners think that I lied to them, but that's not my intent. My hope is that they will see me for who I am in that moment, without additional biases related to history or position.

Why is this such a big deal to me? Because what we do for a living is just a small part of who we are. Granted, it is a large part of our time, as many of us work eight- to nine-hour days outside of our homes, but that doesn't mean it's a large part of our story. One thing I've noticed is that, when I do reply with a truthful answer about what I do for a living, the conversation usually gets cut short, whether intentionally or not.

There's very little probing of who I am beyond the role I've described. This makes it seem to me like a dead-end question.

Now, of course, there are some folks who have become their jobs. I was one of them, or at least I came dangerously close to becoming one of them. They're pretty conversant when it comes to speaking about their industry and their competitors and their products. But you almost have to pull them to the topic of family. I used to work with a guy who, whenever I called him, would immediately dive into financial results and what was going on in the market, no matter when he picked up the phone.

I'd listen and then try moving on with, "That's good to hear. How's your family?"

He'd reply, "Oh, you know, they're fine. The kids are great." There'd be maybe twenty seconds of genuine connection before he'd go back to hitting the work notes.

I once gave a presentation in which I asked, "Who are you?" It sounds like a simple question on the surface, but it opens the door to so many ideas and topics. Our son, Mike, who was at the presentation, wrote on his index card, "A skier." At the time, he was skiing 160 to 180 days a year, so his statement didn't seem inaccurate. But it surprised me because, of all the ways I thought of him at the time, simply labeling him "a skier" never occurred to me.

Part of the reason his answer surprised me is because another question came to me: *What happens when he can no longer ski?* I wondered who he would become then or if he would see even more of himself. Perhaps he would see the person I see, who is a friend to many, loyal, truthful, creative, and heartfelt—uncommon!

Christine

If we don't get to know people very well by asking what they do for work, what should we ask them? There's a lot of options. I've found that you can tell a lot about people from their hobbies. The things people like to do outside of their daily work is becoming more and more diverse, and more interesting!

I once discovered that a previous coworker of mine was really into archaeological digs and had assisted with a few in Idaho. How fun! It seemed so foreign to me but, at the same time, contained a component everyone can relate to, like contemplating our ancestors. Asking "What do you like to do for fun?" invites a more informal yet engaging conversation in this way.

One fruitful topic my husband and I stumbled upon in the past few years is, oddly enough, brunch. Portland is known for its food, and its obsession with late-morning dining is legendary. There's a famous skit in the TV series *Portlandia* in which the producers of the show pay homage to this particular obsession.

Locals aren't too fond of the skit, but it's so true. This obsession with brunch has made it nearly impossible to find a table without having to weigh the amazing taste of the food against the probability of having to wait in line for an hour or two! That's why, when I meet new people in Portland, I like to ask them (1) if they know of a good spot for brunch on the weekends and (2) if they know of a good spot for brunch on the weekends *without* a line! It seems to be something all Portlanders are eager to gripe about, so it's a fun way to bond that's unique to the region.

The simple brunch question spurred my coworkers into conversation, with six of our team members going back and forth about the best and worst brunch places. One thing became another, and the next thing we knew, we were collaborating on a sophisticated spreadsheet charting not just the best brunch places in Portland but the tops for any food and drink. We had a blast trading comments and additions to the list, so much so that it forged a closer connection among us.

All that to say that I do my best to make conversations more organic by steering away from my career and, instead, asking people about their interests or topics we might have in common. I feel like the conversation flows better that way. But that's not to say I go in with preset questions in my head. Doing so runs the risk of creating awkward pauses in conversations.

Another reason I avoid talking about work is because I've experienced it the other way around when Cameron and I are in social situations with medical school folks. People will come up to me and, right off the bat, ask if I work in the medical field. It doesn't really matter to them which branch of that field, I don't think, but they're looking to see if I have a common experience with which they can commiserate. The problem is that when I inevitably tell them that I don't work in medicine, the conversation becomes stunted. Like Dad mentioned, biases form about who I am since I don't have the same experience.

This is why I never want to assume or put people in a box. Their work might not have anything to do with who they are. I've held jobs that I feel do not reflect who I am as a person. Sure, there's a piece of my personality, values, and life in every job I take on, but it isn't all of me. We Americans tend to put such a high importance on job titles and what we do to make money. We live to work versus work to live. By asking what someone does for a living, we're continuing that feedback loop, and we're removing the *human* aspect of a conversation. Asking what someone does for work can sometimes pull out something relatable between two people, but it shouldn't be the first thing we chat about.

I truly live out this approach in my personal life. I don't even know most of my closest friends' job titles or where they work. We all generally know what each other does to earn a living wage, but we rarely discuss the mundane details of job titles, job functions, or places of work.

Sometimes we find ourselves working at jobs we like and that are necessary for making ends meet, but they don't exactly fulfill our career dreams. Right after college, I got a part-time job serving beer at a brewery. I loved my team, and I really liked the company, but I wasn't proud of serving beer. Don't mistake what I'm saying as disdain for the job. That's not it at all. But there I was, a new college graduate, not using my hard-earned degree to make my career, and I didn't see myself as helping the greater good.

As a result, whenever anyone would ask me what I did for a living, I'd try to make an excuse: "Oh, it's just temporary," or "Yeah, I just graduated, and this isn't what I'm hoping to do." I tried to downplay the job because I found the role embarrassing when related to my expectations for myself.

The goal is always to deepen the relationship, whether it's someone you've known for years or someone new to you. Speaking of new, that's a great way to invite deeper conversation: "What's new?" When I made a habit of asking others this question, I found out all kinds of things—friends of mine were going to become uncles and aunts, another person had recently spent time in her hometown after a long absence, and another was planning a lot of travel during the summer.

In one of our Quotes of the Day, Dad and I talked about having to put this continual effort into relationships, while never settling for what's easy:

Good morning, Darling! Happy Hump Day.
Here is your QoD:

Love moves without an agenda. It just moves because that is its nature to move.

—Adyashanti [17]

Adyashanti is a spiritual teacher hailing from the San Francisco Bay Area. He gives talks and leads retreats around the world, and he's written numerous books. This is the first time we have heard from this gentleman!

I think Adya describes unconditional love well, especially in the first sentence: "without an agenda." Having been, most of my life, a person who loves an agenda, this brings clarity for me that an agenda is often about the agenda maker. Or, in my case, the need for control. Granted, there are many times an agenda is simply respectful. The important question is: Why do I have an agenda? If it's for control, then it's not about love and respect. Our friend above nails it. When I don't have an agenda, then it is more out of love—no strings attached, no ulterior motive.

The last line is powerful: "that is its nature to move." To me, this means I act out of love, no other reason. No other agenda. Expecting nothing in return. When I think of those types of actions, it warms my heart and puts a smile on my face!

I love you more than all the movement that is created by love.

Moving Papa

Hey, Daddio!

I agree—love really should be given and received without strings, conditions, or agendas! We shouldn't give love expecting something in return; we should give love as just part of our human nature AND because it's something we WANT to do. It isn't transactional. It isn't something you can turn on and off when it's convenient.

I'm lucky to have grown up with a family that shows me unconditional love. It saddens me to think that there are families out there without that.

I think this quote also pertains to an overarching theme we've touched on many times—as humans, we're intended to be together, to be in relationships, and to be in community. If we love WITH conditions, it's going against our human nature!

> I love you more than all of the ways we can show others we care!
>
> *Christine is Caring*

Tom

There's so much more we can do and ask beyond the mundane to deepen our connections with each other. I'm always trying to engage my curiosity when I'm talking to others, because I know I should be focusing on them and who they are versus steering the discussion to myself. "What did you learn from that experience? Tell me more about that situation? Why do you think I asked that question? How does that still impact you today?"

I had to learn active listening along the way, which harkens back to my earlier mention of being present during the dialogue. Repeating some of what others say back to them lets them know they were heard, which is good, but it still feels a bit mechanical.

Thanks to the training I did with Therese for a good ten years, I always want to get closer to the heart. As far as I'm concerned, she's the undisputed champion of heartfelt listening.

Her approach to questions and conversation went beyond active listening. She would drop bombshells like: "What's your heart telling you? If you were to quiet your intellect, what would your heart say? As a child, what would you ask?"

I found that her questions took me to a different place, one that encouraged me to reach for the heart and expose more emotion, to care for others and extend to them tremendous empathy. This isn't to say that taking this approach is all joy and happiness. Inviting deeper conversation means that you'll inevitably unearth difficult topics and powerful emotions.

I was once asked in a meeting, "Tom, how come you never get upset?"

I replied, "My dad says that if you get upset, you lose."

But the questioner pressed in: "I believe there's more to it than that." She was right. My mother's fits of rage made me fear expressing anger in any form. I was afraid that I would skip frustration or anger and go directly to rage, and I didn't want anyone to experience that behavior from me.

Often our first authentic question cracks the surface, while the second or third one usually penetrates it. The result is silence or occasionally tears. These questions sometimes lead to places that aren't fun but that help people grow past experiences they are harboring inside. That is exactly what happened to me. Suddenly, tears were flowing, and I was confessing, "I've never shared that with anyone before."

When others share their feelings, I feel blessed to know they were comfortable enough with me to express their emotions. I was just the person who asked the right question at the right moment to open the door. It's even more vital at those times for me to be there for them, to recognize the special spot they're in, and to let them speak from their vulnerability.

There's always going to be a risk in pursuing genuine relationships. But it's important to take that risk, because the regret of not going deep is far worse, as I made sure to express to Christine.

Good morning, Darling! TGIM!!

It was so wonderful being with you yesterday! Thank you so much for coming home!

Here is your QoD:

Not everything that is faced can be changed, but nothing can be changed until it is faced.

—James Baldwin

James Baldwin was an American writer and civil rights activist. He garnered acclaim for his work across several forms, including essays, novels, plays, and poems.

What I love about this quote is its simplicity and candor: you can't change everything, and you won't know what you can change until you try. Whoa, basically this is saying to me: stop talking and get doing. This is so true for me. So many times and still today, I can get stopped or slowed by logic that says something can't be done or is almost impossible, so why try. And MANY, MANY more times than not, I am able to have an impact I thought I couldn't. The most important part of my efforts has to do with scope. What is it I am trying to change? For example, I cannot change what is happening with our government: too big a scope, too many moving parts. However, I can change things through something with a much smaller scope, like Fellowship of Companies for Christ International, which will impact my life and others. AND its impact on business over time could start to impact Washington. But I cannot start there.

Also, there is part of this quote that is assumed: "faced." What does that mean? One and done? Not likely! To me that means being all in on what is required to bring about that change, which usually is an ongoing effort, ongoing commitment. AND most importantly, to persevere through the most challenging times, because any worthwhile change will have its point where you want to give up, in essence confirm that it could not be done. But I have to push through that to see the light!

I love you more than all that is possible when it is thought not!

Possible Papa

Hey, Pops!

Sorry for my tardiness! It's so great to be at home. I truly do love spending time with you and mom!

Man oh man! There was a lot here for you. Thank you for sharing! This quote makes me think about my schooling and sustainability. There's a lot of issues out there in the world that need attention. However, we can't tackle everything all at the same time. Even one issue has multiple steps that need to take place! It's not a catch-all solution in 99% of instances. Additionally, in terms of environmental issues, we kind of don't know until we try. The unfortunate part is that, more times than not, there are unintended consequences to what we implement that we don't know the full impact of until many years later! It definitely seems complex! So it seems perfect to marry this quote with sustainability and climate change.

I agree with you about the impact! I do agree that before I start a project or anything new, I'm doubtful about the outcome, the impact on me and others. But once I take that first leap, everything becomes easier, and my impact becomes more apparent!

I love you more than all of the ways we can just get started!

Christine's READY ... SET ... GO!

Tom (continued)

This email exchange reveals how important risk is for living a full life, including taking risks in my relationships to be real, honest, and vulnerable. This brings me back, inevitably, to trust. Trust keeps a relationship together by building an environment in which both people are comfortable conversing on deeper topics, both the lighthearted and the solemn.

QUESTIONS FOR REFLECTION

How do you feel when others share their hearts with you? How do you feel when you share yours with them? How can you develop more authentic, heartfelt relationships with the people in your life? How would your life change if you were to accomplish this goal?

Never Underestimate Your Impact

Tom

The best advice I can give is never to underestimate your impact. I know that I have several times!

I used to tell myself that people really didn't care what I had to say. Then, months later, someone would come up to me and repeat something I had said in a meeting or a social setting. I was amazed.

How you have impact is completely up to you. I chose to send daily quotes about leadership, values, and heart. There are myriad ways to reach out to the person with whom you'd like to reconnect. Pick the one that works for you, which will make it easier and more likely to continue.

Long before I sent Christine that first Quote of the Day, I took to mailing physical cards. A fellow I'd worked with had been sending handwritten notes to people he knew, whether it was a full-length letter or a simple greeting on a sticky note. He was convinced that there was power behind the physical written word, no matter what form. "All it takes is a couple of sentences," he'd say.

My skepticism initially kept me away from following his advice, until a few months later, when I pondered his words again. *Why not give it a try?*

I sent a handwritten note to a mentor of mine, thanking him for all his time, effort, and patience. I didn't expect a reply, but the next time we saw each other, he made a point of expressing his appreciation. Then, about a month later, our paths crossed again, and he added, "Thanks again for that note, Tom. I keep it in my sock drawer."

That's all it took. Writing notes has now become one of my favorite relationship tools, and it doesn't even have to be a birthday, anniversary, or other special occasion. I have a stash of blank white cards folded in half and a small desktop photo printer. All it takes is penning a few lines that express my care for the other person, printing off a meaningful photo, usually of me and that person at a special place, and gluing the picture on the front of the card.

None of that, in and of itself, is special. It's a simple, repeatable set of steps I use to let my family and friends know I love them. There's no need to make the maintenance of these connections complex and onerous. Why make expressing your heart something you don't look forward to doing?

I have to fight against my tendency to overthink what should be very basic, very caring gestures.

Christine

I keep coming back to the idea of awareness. It's been a difficult challenge for me, ever since my early college days, when I would engage in conversations by talking about myself. I assumed it was the best way to get people talking about themselves, but it turned out to have the opposite effect. I had to start being more inquisitive and less in presentation mode.

Considering impact has forced me to battle my homebody status. I'm much more comfortable staying home and relaxing, but I know that turning down invitations to social outings or long weekends can keep relationships stagnant. My anxieties plague me. *What am I going to say? What if the conversation turns to awkward silence? How would I fix it?*

I've been letting go of those worries and stepping out more, trying to let myself be in the moment with others instead of losing myself in the future. It's time to set aside the phone. And I feel like it's working.

Cameron and I recently went to dinner with friends. I made a concerted effort to ignore the clock so I wouldn't tell myself, "Okay, Christine, you're done for the evening." The restaurant was artificially lit and decorated with plants to make it seem like it was outside. It felt like time was frozen. I think we arrived around 6:30. Hours passed as we ate, drank, and enjoyed warm and funny conversation. When I finally did check the time, it was nearly midnight.

The realization was almost as joyous as the fellowship we'd exchanged. I'd set aside my anxieties, which weren't rooted in reality, and had opened myself up to a new approach to the relationships I hold dear. I would have missed those engaging and deep conversations if I'd held back and made excuses for not attending what turned out to be a great evening spent with friends.

I've always considered myself a people pleaser. I like to keep peace, but more importantly, I like to keep those around me happy. I'd love for my impact on others to be centered around kindness, humor, and thoughtfulness. Will it work out that way in the end? At this point, I don't know, but there's hope for the future in that respect.

The Quotes of the Day have helped me take bigger, bolder risks in my care and feeding of these relationships. Dad's curiosity leads him to ask wonderful open-ended, non-leading questions. His impact on my personality is real. A short time ago, I met a couple from Baltimore. Based on media reports I've seen and comments I've heard about the city, I have developed preconceived ideas about what it might be like to live there. But instead of asking, "Did you like Baltimore?" I said, "So, tell me about Baltimore." Initiating the dialogue in this way took my opinion out of the equation, and I think this helped me approach the conversation without my bias, allowing for a more authentic exchange of ideas. It's an important lesson I've definitely taken to heart.

Tom

My daily interaction with Christine through the Quotes has been a godsend. From a practical standpoint, it has helped me transition to retirement and provided a structure in an often structureless world. It also allowed me to share some of my work experiences to help with the withdrawal from work, in essence providing a glide path to the next chapter of my life.

But most importantly, it has invited me to be more open and vulnerable, trusting Christine with the revelation of my true self, with more of an emphasis on the Real Tom than on Dad Tom or Business Tom. The impact of our expanded relationship has been calming, making me more available, compassionate, and authentic.

I'd like to share a few final words of encouragement with you.

First, don't wait. You must take the initiative to reach out to others if you want to improve the relationships already dear to you. It all starts with the steps you take. If you wait on the other people, they may never know how important they are to you.

You have to choose to make this gesture because you care for the person, not because you expect a response. That can't be the deciding factor. When I started sending Christine the Quotes of the Day, I didn't press the return key and sit back with my arms folded, thinking, "All right, if she's not interested in this, I won't try it again."

Instead, I was looking to start a relationship. I wanted to offer safety and security for Christine during a time of great uncertainty, with quotes from people whose words and thoughts captured what I thought were valuable lessons in leadership and life. But those emails weren't sent with the expectation that I would get anything back.

Let unconditional love influence your decision. Leave conditional love by the wayside. Don't place any expectations on your loved ones. Your guide should be your heart, not logic.

On the other hand, you shouldn't just wing it. Be intentional with what you do. Be able to answer these questions— if not initially, then in the long term:

- Why am I doing this?

- Who is it really for?

- How often will I do it?

- How will I know the impact?

Our words carry tremendous weight, and not just in our direct conversations with others. People see themselves in our stories. They start to reflect and think, and the next thing you know, the story we've told, the vulnerable side we've shown, has a greater impact than we ever thought possible.

This has been a long journey for me. The old me would tell people how limited my time was, implying that my resources were finite and they were lucky to receive a portion of them. The three-minute timer stands in my office to this day as a reminder. What's changed is my gradual embrace of patience and curiosity. There's less of me judging what people have to say and more of me asking them questions about how an incident made them feel or what an experience taught them.

This is about forging connections between two people during moments that could otherwise pass you by. So the next time you're in a social situation and a stranger starts with, "What do you do for a living?" or the next time you think, "I haven't spoken to my daughter in a long time, and I miss being a closer part of her life," that's the time to take action.

Take the risk. Open yourself and truly listen to what the other person has to say. You'll find your love for each other lasting much longer than any of the words you exchange. Now that's impact!

I Love You More Than...

Quotes of the Day

The following Quote of the Day emails stand alone—no introduction, no backstory. They convey exactly how we shared our perspectives over the last four years. We hope you find value in this peek into our attempts to form a more authentic relationship. May they resonate not only with your mind but even more with your heart. Enjoy!

—Tom and Christine

TWO HANDS

Good morning, Darling!
Here is your QoD for TGIM!

As you grow older, you will discover that you have two hands, one for helping yourself, the other for helping others.

—Audrey Hepburn

Audrey's got it going on!

Another great confirmation that we are here to help others! *And* it is important that we help ourselves. We have so much capability, and yet, at times, we can choose not to use our abilities because we are tired or frustrated or playing the victim. And more than I would like to admit, I usually neglect myself with some form of errant rationalization. You are much better at taking care of yourself than I was at twenty-five! An order of magnitude better!

Fortunately, I am still able to live up to my capability! As Uncle Joe would say, "Slow but sure!"

Have a great Monday.

Love you more than all the capabilities we have!

Capable Carmazzi

Good morning, Dad!

Wow, isn't that the truth! I know I also get into a selfish state of mind, especially once I get busy. I begin to tell myself that I only have time to focus on myself or the things that pertain to me versus those that others might need help with! However, there is always time to help loved ones! It's interesting how you notice you neglect yourself. I have definitely noticed that from you!

Where I'm the opposite way, I hope that shifts with time.

I love you more than all of the Olympic medals given out over time!

Xoxo

Christine's Capable of Giving More

DEPTH OF FRIENDSHIP

Good morning, Darling!

Today, I am the one who is late!

Here is your QoD:

True happiness consists not in the multitude of friends, but in their worth and choice.

—Ben Johnson [18]

Ben was an American film and television actor, stunt-man, and world champion rodeo cowboy. Whoa, Nelly!

I love this quote because it makes a lot of sense for many things in life. It is not the numbers but the quality. Who we choose to spend our time with says a lot about what we value. I don't have many friends, but those I have are ones I trust, have deep-rooted values, and bring happiness.

Interestingly, if I had more friends, I am not sure how that would turn out. I feel, at some point, I would not be able to have the depth of friendship to bring the happiness I would want. Friendship takes time for me. I do like the challenge of determining the point of diminishing returns. I know I have room for more friends—probably not twenty, but maybe five?

I love you more than all the joy our friendships bring.

Friendly Father

Hi, Dad!

Whoa! This is very fitting. As Cameron and I decide where we want to get married, a big topic of discussion is whether or not our friends will travel if we get married in Chicago. My point of view is that everyone who we *really* want there (the day would not be the same without them) would travel from Oregon or the West Coast to Chicago. I do not need five hundred people at our wedding, only those who would make a wonderful impact and would make both of us very happy to share the day with. I have never had *heaps* of friends, just a few who I really care about and try hard to keep relationships going. I, like you, do not think I would do myself or the other person justice if I tried to divide my quality time between more than twenty people.

I love you more than our ability to choose words wisely!

Teensie Loves Quality Time

TREATING OTHERS

Good morning, Darling!

Here is your QoD:

154

The true measure of a man is how he treats someone who can do him absolutely no good.

—Ann Landers [19]

This is very true for me. I used to take candidates to lunch or dinner to see how they treated the waitstaff. Or I'd have them walk through the plant to see how they addressed the hourly team. Too many times, they ignored those folks when a simple smile would have been impactful.

It's funny, when taking my morning walk, how some folks offer a quick hello while others offer no reply. I believe all interaction is important. All people are important and children of God. We're meant to be in relationship! Oxytocin baby!

I love you more than all that happens when we treat people with respect.

Respectful Papa

Good morning, Daddio!

Amen on this quote! It is a huge sign of character when you watch people interact with waitstaff or anyone in the service industry. Same with people who tip. People who tip someone in the service industry well, compared to those who do not, are usually much kinder in general. The BLM movement is also very telling—*all* people are children of God and, therefore, should be treated as such!

I love you more than all of the ways we can be kind to those around us!

Xoxo 4 EVA!

Christine is Leading with Kindness

Truth—Fragment by Fragment

Good morning, Darling!!

Here is your QoD:

There are very few human beings who receive the truth, complete and staggering, by instant illumination. Most of them acquire it fragment by fragment, on a small scale, by successive developments, cellularly like a laborious mosaic.

—Anais Nin [20]

Whoa! This is deep! Anais was a French-Cuban-American [writer] who died in 1977. No doubt a deep thinker!

I believe this quote is true. I've encountered several folks who I believed had epiphanies, only to realize their behavior had not changed. So, I see this as the difference between *knowing* and *doing*. Folks may have an illumination in the moment and indicate such; however, the behavior does not change immediately. Only through subsequent reinforcement does the acquisition occur.

The closest I've come to experiencing this was the first time I saw the Toyota Production System. I was amazed by the system and pursued it as best I could from that point on. On the other hand, I have been told several times that I can be distant and mechanical (i.e., I see figures versus faces). I believe this to be true, yet it has been a "laborious mosaic."

I love you more than all that becomes possible when change has deep roots.

Illuminated Papa (but still painting the Mosaic)

Good morning, Dad!

Whoa! You're right—Anais was a deep thinker! And I agree with him! Unfortunately, I have seen too many people at my young age who believe that things will just fall from the sky for them or—like Anais is saying—they will receive gifts and ideas through instant illumination! You must *work* for that stuff, hello!

I like how you worded the actionability/difference between the two. You're right—one is thinking about it (which can happen rather instantly) and the other is going through the ins and outs of an idea and actually putting it into place! Super cool. This helps differentiate people!

I'm glad you're still painting the mosaic. I've liked being a part of your journey so far! I have a *long* way to go! But I have enjoyed sitting in on conferences and getting inspired by seeing what others have done! Looking forward to even more as time goes on!

I love you more than all of the ways we can put our puzzles together, piece by piece, to create a masterpiece.

Novice Painter Carmazzi

SEEING IS TREATING

Good morning, Darling! TGIF!!

Here is your QoD:

The way you see people is the way you treat them, and the way you treat them is what they become.

—*Johann Wolfgang von Goethe* [21]

157

Johann Wolfgang von Goethe was primarily a writer, one of Germany's most influential, but he was also a scientist, statesman, and theater director.

This quote is so true to me. Time and time again, I notice the impact I have on others. How I "see people" is driven by how I am doing. When I am full of energy and accepting, guess what—I see people differently. When I am grumpy and distant, guess what I see. And I know how I see people shows in my interactions, and they respond accordingly. Granted, there are times when others are in their own world and my behavior has little impact. However, I know I have more impact than I want to admit. Try it sometime and notice how you show up and impact others.

Actually, I love that impact or responsibility. Just think of the impact I could have if I showed up in every interaction in an accepting mood. Wow! I know I would have impacted a lot more lives. As you know, I am not a big fan of some folks. And when I've seen them, I have been very quick in my dialogue and moved on. What would have been different if I had truly engaged? What wisdom could I have acquired? What impact could I have had? I will never know, unless I see them differently!

I love you more than all the benefits of "seeing" people as God created them versus how I have "created" them.

See-the-Truth Carmazzi

Good afternoon, Dad!

Holy cow! How special is this quote! I completely agree with you—when I am full of energy and wanting to be present, I believe my impact on others is much greater than when I am tired or not wanting to converse. It is challenging for me to always be on. I'm realizing as I get older that socializing really wears me out! I am able to have high energy, good conversation, etc., but afterwards, I'm drained. If I have big social events day after day after day, I tend to be less engaging and present than if I have a couple days to recuperate. If only I took the perspective of others, I believe I would be quick to change my attitude!

For example, last night we met friends for dinner—a dinner that lasted until 10:15 p.m.! I knew I had a busy day today, and I knew Cam had a lot of things to do before he could go to bed. Instead of fully enjoying my time at dinner, all I could think about was how late a night we would have. I'm sure that came across in my dialogue with friends, and I know I could have been a better friend if I had let go of those inner thoughts.

I'm curious about your note regarding people you are not a fan of. At a certain level, I think it is great to continue to push forward with a cordial relationship, but at other times, it is fair to say enough is enough and move along. That's very kind of you to reflect and try another avenue! That's more than what I would do.

I love you more than all of the learnings I would acquire if I stayed out of my own head!

Christine is Focusing on Learning

CREATE YOUR OWN OPPORTUNITIES

Good afternoon, Darling!

If opportunity doesn't knock, build a door.

—*Milton Berle*

159

Milton was a comedian from years ago. I love this quote because of its proactive nature. It is quite clever in the way it says that if opportunity doesn't knock, then create the way for it to knock. Don't improve your hearing; improve your preparation and the ability for it to show up.

For me, this describes my experience when I first went to Cooper Industries in Houston, Texas. I was on the corporate audit staff. But I wanted to get to one of the divisions and off the corporate staff. I knew the division was where all the cool stuff happened. My boss told me that was a possible career path. However, as I asked around, I learned no one had ever taken it. So, I "built a door"! Whenever I visited divisions to audit them, I would tell the head of finance that a great career path for an auditor was to become a member of the division team and that is why I had come to Cooper. Well, guess what! Someone knocked, and your mom and I moved to Springfield, Ohio!

I love you more than all the knocks that will occur in our lives!

Knock, Knock, who's there Carmazzi

Hey, Dad,

Oh, so true! This quote is very *inviting* of success, not *expecting*!

Your story is incredible! And a perfect example of how you worked hard with what you had and didn't stand by idly! For me, a big door-creation moment was with the ASU School of Sustainability's internship program. No one in the school's history had gone out of state and completed a nontraditional internship like I had! I kept sending emails and making phone calls until one clicked! Booyah!

I love you more than all of the doors we'll create!

Xoxox!

It's me! Ready for action!

COMFORT VS. TRUTH

Good morning, Darling!

Here is your QoD:

If you look for truth, you may find comfort in the end; if you look for comfort you will not get either comfort or truth— only soft soap and wishful thinking to begin, and in the end, despair.

—C. S. Lewis [22]

Whoa! C. S. is on it this morning! Recently, much of my reading has been about the challenges. Hmm ... and here we have it again. Granted, I have had some very recent challenges, *and* I find this perspective rather comforting (but not comfortable)—a pure invitation away from victimhood. An invitation to character, maturity, and respect. Timing is perfect.

Also, I find that, when I seek some form of comfort beyond a moment or a day, it gets lost in the challenges. Not complaining, just noticing. Maybe I was not built for comfort. Maybe none of us were! We are made to be growing and learning in search of the truth as to why we are here. Directionally, we all know, and what is our version of that!

I love you more than all the facets of the Learning Zone.

Uncomfortable Carmazzi

161

Good morning, Dad!

Whoa! I like to see this quote also pointing to the importance of having an open mind. If you go into a situation with a bias or searching for something specific, you are losing out on obtaining the info that is right in front of you. Example: If you want the truth to be one thing (comfort) and you go about your life trying to prove that thing right, then you're losing out on comfort and truth and cheating yourself!

Your note about how none of us are made for comfort is spot-on! We were designed to have shelter, food, and basic needs, but never comfort! We've adapted to enjoy and build comfort, but we're not hardwired for it. Great point!

I love you more than all of the boundaries that can be stretched and molded when we live outside of our comfort zones!

Christine Isn't Cozy

THE POWER OF AWARENESS

Good morning, Darling! Hope your camping trip was wonderful!

Here is your QoD:

The real voyage of discovery consists not in seeking new landscapes, but in having new eyes.

—Marcel Proust [23]

Marcel Proust was an influential twentieth-century French novelist, critic, and essayist.

What I love about this quote is that discovery is always present. It is only a matter of how aware I am in the moment. From conversations to environments, I can think of many times when I failed to capture much of what there was to see or hear. I have shared many stories of my leadership journey, which are highlighted in this quote. I can also think of McGregor Bay. There is so much here, just outside our cabin, that I have not explored. So much beauty, so much of God's creation!

It's funny how we did so much on all our vacations, and yet we just scratched the surface!

I love you more than all of my life yet to be discovered!

Discovering Daddy!

Good morning, Dad!

Camping was *great*! A whole lot of biking, hiking, swimming, kayaking, etc.! It was really wonderful to spend so much time outdoors. :-)

And wow! Yes, this quote is so pertinent today and every day! Even when you are visiting a place you've seen before, there is still so much you can discover if you take time to look for the discoveries! You brought up the example of McGregor Bay. Think about all of those islands we've never set foot on! There are *tons* there that we may never see, even though we've visited the area before. I have a feeling I'll notice a lot of new things I haven't seen before when I am up there next summer, given I will have "new eyes."

This idea can also be translated to a new employee—they often see flaws that existing employees haven't seen before. They are able to look at areas with new eyes and point out problems that have gone unnoticed. Pretty cool stuff!

I love you more than all of the hours I wish I could be at McGregor Bay!

xoxox!

Teensie Is Wide-Eyed

REAL COURAGE

Good morning, Darling!

Here is your QoD:

Real courage is when you know you're licked before you begin, but you begin anyway and see it through no matter what.

—Harper Lee [24]

Nelle Harper Lee was an American novelist best known for her 1960 novel *To Kill a Mockingbird.* It won the 1961 Pulitzer Prize. If you have not read this book, put it on your list!

I see this quote a little like the difference between commitment and devotion. Commitment is about the intellect; it is logical, linear, rational, and tangible. You can quickly see if something makes sense, and if it doesn't, you don't do it. Devotion is about the heart, which tends to be nonlinear, sometimes irrational, and many times intangible. Same with courage—you are stepping into the unknown, and it scares you. Or what you do know scares you, but you proceed anyway for the greater good. You test your reality. You are prepared for the possibility that it is true, and you are prepared if it isn't.

Courage, in this case, sounds a little more intellectual and like blind commitment. Actually, I believe the quote is not finished. I would add, "Because you believe," leaving the interpretation of *believe* to the reader. For me, *believe* means that I know things happen for a reason—I know that God put me here, at this time, for a reason. With this belief, I step forward. Would I be scared? Yes, but that's part of living!

Several times in my life, I have been told that a certain course of action was not possible or that it could not be done a particular way, yet I proceeded. Some courage and some ego, but I have been blessed up to this point. The key point of this quote is to trust yourself and God. We are not an accident!

I love you more than all the courage in the world to step into the arena to make things better!

Courage-seeking Carmazzi

Good afternoon, Courage Seeking!

This is so cool, and your distinction between commitment and devotion is very pertinent. I think that our commitment to things is all context dependent. Whether or not we see sticky situations through to the end depends on what that thing is. If it is something I do not care about or that doesn't impact others, I am less likely to stick around when things get challenging. However, if that ugly situation has components that mean a lot to me, I'll stick around! It is also worth noting that not everyone has the courage to stick around when times get tough. This relates back to personal character and heart.

You are an inspiration for sticking out the tough times and doing what was deemed impossible! I am grateful to know someone as impactful as you are!

I love you more than all of the positive potential in all of us!

Christine is Making Things Happen

Thwarting Anger

Good morning, Darling! TGIF.

Here is your QoD:

An angry man opens his mouth and shuts his eyes.

—Cato the Elder [25]

Cato the Elder, born in 234 BC, was a Roman soldier and senator who wrote a history of Rome titled *Origines*.

Wow! This is so true for me! When I get upset, I go internal. I am not considering the environment or the feelings of the person I am in dialogue with. I am purely in the fight-or-flight mode. This can also occur when I am not in the dialogue of the moment. It can also happen when I am fearful of something. When I was working, if I needed to address something in the plant that worried me, I'd make a beeline to that location and completely ignore all external happenings along the way. I can only imagine the message that sent to all who saw me!

Today, I am getting better at recognizing when I am "spooling up" and then creating space. Yesterday, I was working on getting the boat insured, a process that has been going on for over a month. I was ready to pop; I was getting angry. I wrote an indignant email, the kind I would normally send, but I stopped myself from sending it. I got up and did the dishes and came back to the email. I changed it to be less angry and more heartfelt. And guess what—the representative responded favorably, and I got the documentation I needed.

I love you more than all the opportunities to bring the heart when the head is saying to "spool up."

Open-eyes Carmazzi

Hey, Dad,

Wow! What a timely quote for your instance yesterday. I'm proud of you for stepping away and coming back to the task with a clear head. Nicely done! I, too, can get riled up, sometimes off of something that isn't very substantial. For me, I'm not quick to turn those emotions of anger off. It's something that I'm working on, but I recognize I have a long way to go. Not only for the sake of my relationships with others but also for the awareness aspect of my life! I'm just now realizing that all of that time I'm angry and unable to cool down, I'm blind to much more around me than I realize. Talk about wasting time that will never come back!

I always like to have the awareness as to *why* I'm getting angry and who is on the receiving end. I like to think of these things in instances of customer service, in particular. I'm thinking about all of the times I've been frustrated with a system, but I'll take it out on the "face" of the system, which is never the answer, and I am trying to move forward in life without anger in those instances!

I love you more than all of the ways we can decrease anger, to be more open and aware of the happiness in life!

Christine Wants to be Happy

A Hand Up Versus a Handout

Good morning, Darling! Here is your QoD:

You cannot help men [or women] permanently by doing for them what they could and should do for themselves.

—William Boetcker [26]

This is powerful! The challenge for me is to know when to help and when to not. In given business situations, I used to think of the Coach, Dictate, or Abdicate triangle. There was a time when I slipped to *abdicate* too much. Consequently, the team was looking for direction that I did not provide, with the belief that I did not want to caretake them. Unfortunately, in hindsight, I believe that was not the best answer. I could have given direction without caretaking.

Another way I have looked at this is the magnitude of risk: safety, financial, emotional. When there is great risk, I tend to dictate; when very little, I will abdicate; and when balanced, I coach. Easy to outline, difficult to do in practice. Yet, that is what leaders get paid to do.

I love you more than all the ways to be impactful in a given situation.

Coaching Carmazzi

Good morning, Dad!

I think this is a great quote from a great leader! I do not think you're alone when it comes to helping people or assisting their journey. It can be beneficial to help people gain skills and lessons so they can take it on later in life.

168

It can also be so helpful to delegate. I think you're right—very few people find this balance with ease, *and* people like yourself were put in the positions that you held because you were able to accomplish a balance. Super cool!

I love you so much!

I miss you, daddio!

Climbing Christine

CAPTURE THE GROWTH FROM YOUR MISTAKES

Good morning, Darling!

Here is a little humor for your QoD:

Experience is the name everyone gives to their mistakes.

—Oscar Wilde [27]

Oscar was a writer and comedian, as you can tell.

And yet there is much truth to his quote. However, I know not all passage of time is about mistakes. I get some stuff right!

His intent, I believe, was humility and awareness. A little reminder about our travel on this journey.

I love you more than all the wonderful things we experience in our lives, including those that in the moment don't appear to be so pleasurable!

Experiencing the journey, Papa

Good afternoon, Dad!

Looks as though we've swapped weather. We are getting some rain here today! I hope you are experiencing a break in the clouds.

An "Amen, Brotha!" experience typically does not come from perfection or from lack of time! It comes with learning lessons—mostly the hard way, I might add! Your point about adding some humor to our journey is perfect. Failing is never fun, nor easy, but it is all part of perfecting the craft of life!

I love you more than all of the opportunities to turn lemons into lemonade!

Christine is Seeking Silver Linings

THE RELATIONSHIP BETWEEN INSPIRATION AND EXECUTION

Good morning, Darling! Happy Hump day!

Here is your QoD:

Without craftsmanship, inspiration is a mere reed shaken in the wind.

—Johannes Brahms [28]

Johannes Brahms was a German composer, pianist, and conductor of the mid-Romantic period.

What I love about this quote is the relationship of inspiration and execution. Many things are started with inspiration; however, they only get brought to reality via execution. Many times, as the execution gets very challenging, I'll return to the inspiration to get the energy to continue. The "craftsmanship" speaks to the quality of the execution. And that is where the inspiration really kicks in.

I can get seduced by "good enough" and then move on to the next inspiration; however, excellence only occurs when the temptation of "good enough" is not accepted and the inspiration returns to achieve excellence. Most recently, this cycle occurs when I am preparing for a facilitation. Since I have done so many of those, it is very easy to say to myself, "This is good enough." However, each facilitation is different, and many times the audience is as well, so my love (inspiration) of facilitation calls me forth to continue to work on the outline until it is worth the endeavor.

I love you more than the power of spirited craftsmanship!

Crafty Carmazzi

Hey, Daddio,

My gosh! Yes, you speak to so many different audiences, from all sorts of backgrounds. You would be challenged to find a one-size-fits-all presentation that speaks to everyone! I love that you're able to adapt and reimagine your original presentation to fit everyone's interests and demographics.

Inspiration comes from many different places for everyone. We also all have diverse skill sets and crafts! I really like this quote because it speaks to the common thread among all of us—we all can get inspired to do more with our talents! And if we choose not to, we're skipping over an opportunity for innovation.

I love you more than all of the ways we can be inspired and act on it!

Christine is Going into Action

WE ARE COMPLETE, JUST AS WE ARE

Good morning, Darling!

Here is your QoD:

You cannot teach a man anything; you can only help him find it within himself.

—Galileo [29]

Hmmm ... this guy had it all together many, many years ago!

What I love about this quote is the belief that we are whole as we are. Therefore, all we have to do is believe that and let it out. I think much of this is true. We are much stronger and capable than we believe, and yet we hold ourselves small. The best leaders, friends, and colleagues are those who see us for who we are and invite the best of us to come out and play.

I do believe we can be taught more than what resides in us. An obvious example is what you learn at school that did not exist within it. But that is more mechanical. Our true power does come from within.

Have a great Tuesday.

I love you more than the unlimited capability that exists within you!

Letting the Soul Appear, Daddy

Good morning, Dad!

Wow—this is empowering stuff! I agree with the notes you have. I think that we can always take in and learn more, but it is how we apply it (which all comes from within) that really matters. I, too, think that genetics, as well as our environment, have an impact on whether or not we know how to unleash our inner knowledge. I know that my high school really pushed kids to unleash their potential, but I have the feeling that was not the case in every public high school in the Chicagoland area! How blessed was I?

I also like your comment regarding our loved ones who invite us to open up and be our authentic selves. They see us in higher regards than we see ourselves—that is a nice reminder not to be so harsh internally and instead be more courageous to show our knowledge and strengths!

I love you more than all of the fireworks that went off this weekend!

Christine's Unleashing Potential

I Love You More Than...

In Closing

We hope you have found reading our book as enjoyable and enlightening as we found the writing of it.

I (Tom) must admit that I initially assumed that the effort of writing it would seem like a chore and we would come to cherish it only after completion. What I have found is quite different. This endeavor has unearthed memories from our lives that we have felt honored to share.

If, in some small way, we have touched your heart, then the book has been a grand success. From the very start, our purpose was to awaken the heart!

With love,
Christine and Tom

I Love You More Than...

About the Authors

Tom Carmazzi had a business career spanning forty-three years! His business journey was like many others', leading with his head before his heart. He focused on the "figures before the faces." However, he reached a point where he knew something was not right. That awareness led him down a path of opening his heart much earlier in relationships with those around him. Tom lives in Chicagoland with his wife, Deb, and they have two adult children. This book brings together some of the wisdom he has acquired over the years through various wake-up calls, heartfelt coaching, and time in the "arena."

CHRISTINE CARMAZZI graduated with a bachelor's degree from Arizona State University in 2018 and is currently working as part of a Supply Chain team for a manufacturing company. She lives in Southern California with her husband, Cameron. She has a passion for sustainability and has been able to deepen that passion throughout her supply chain-based career. Christine enjoys numerous outdoor sports: hiking, skiing, fishing, kayaking, rock climbing, and running—especially if she is joined by her family and friends! Her happy place is in McGregor Bay, Ontario, which offers peace, connection with nature, and facilitation of new memories with her loved ones.

About Renown Publishing

Renown Publishing is the proud publishing imprint of Speak It To Book, an elite team of publishing professionals devoted to helping you shape, write, and share your book. Renown has written, edited, and worked on hundreds of books (including New York Times, Wall Street Journal, and USA Today best-sellers, and the #1 book on all of Amazon).

We believe authentic stories are the torch of change-makers, and our mission is to collaborate with purpose-driven authors to create societal impact and redeem culture.

If you're the founder of a purpose-driven company, visit RenownPublishing.com.

If you're an aspiring author, visit SpeakItToBook.com.

I Love You More Than...

Notes

1. Thatcher, Margaret. "Remarks on Becoming Prime Minister (St. Francis's Prayer)." In *Thatcher Archive: Transcript.* May 4, 1979. https://www.margaretthatcher.org/document/104078.

A quotation of St. Francis of Assisi.

2. Watkinson, William Lonsdale. "Sermon XIV: The Invincible Strategy, Romans: xii, 21." *The Supreme Conquest and Other Sermons Preached in America.* Fleming H. Revell Company, 1907, p 217–218.

3. Churchill, Winston. "The Gift of a Common Tongue." Speech given at Harvard University, Boston, MA, September 6, 1943. In *Resources: Speeches.* International Churchill Society. https://winstonchurchill.org/resources/speeches/1941-1945-war-leader/the-gift-of-a-common-tongue/.

4. Newman, Ben. *Uncommon Leadership.* Per Capita Publishing, 2021.

5. Swindoll, Charles. "The God of the Impossible: Matthew 19:26." *The Swindoll Study Bible.* Tyndale, 2017, p. 1,170.

6. The brief biography included in many of my (Tom's) original emails borrowed heavily from the Wikipedia article on the relevant person.

7. Bacon, Francis. "Essays Civil and Moral: LII. Of Ceremonies and Respects." *The Works of Francis Bacon, Baron of Verulam, Viscount St. Albans, and Lord High Chancellor of England.* Vol. 2. W. Baynes and Son, 1824, p. 378.

8. Boetcker, William J. H. *The Ten Cannots.* 1916.

This quotation has often been misattributed to Abraham Lincoln (including in our original email exchange).

9. This quotation is popularly attributed to Lewis Carroll, but the actual origin is unknown.

10. Groeschel, Craig. *Lead Like It Matters: 7 Leadership Principles for a Church That Lasts.* Zondervan, 2022. p. 81.

11. Newman, *Uncommon Leadership.*

12. Or, "Love can begin at once where knowledge ends."

Aquinas, Thomas. *Summa Theologica of St. Thomas Aquinas,* Part 2. Translated by Fathers of the English Dominican Province. R&T Washbourne, 1917, p. 364.

13. Jampolsky, Gerald. *Love Is Letting Go of Fear.* Bantam, 1985, p. 65.

14. Watkinson, "Sermon XIV."

Adlai Stevenson incorporated a version of this saying, which may be attributed to Watkinson or to an ancient Chinese proverb, in his eulogy of Eleanor Roosevelt.

15. Covey, Stephen R. *7 Habits of Highly Effective People.* Free Press, 2004, p. 46.

16. Twain, Mark. *Extracts from Adam's Diary: Translated from the Original MS.* Harper & Bros.,1904, p. 45.

17. Adyashanti. *Emptiness Dancing.* Sounds True, 2006.

18. Johnson, Ben. *Cynthia's Revel,* 3.4.104–106. In Ben Johnson, *The Works of Ben Johnson: In Six Volumes; Adorn'd with Cuts.* J. Walthoe, M. Wotton, J. Nicholson, J. Sprint, G. Conyers, B. Tooke, D. Midwinter, T. Ballard, B. Cowse, F. Tonson, and W. Innys, 1716, p. 321.

19. Forbes, Malcolm S. *The Sayings of Chairman Malcolm: The Capitalist's Handbook.* Harper & Row, 1978.

Though Landers and others, some much earlier, have offered similar statements, Malcolm Forbes was credited with this precursor to Landers's version in 1972: "You can easily judge the character of others by how they treat those who can do nothing for them or to them." For reference, see:

"You Can Easily Judge the Character of a Man by How He Treats Those Who Can Do Nothing for Him." Quote Investigator. October 28, 2011. https://quoteinvestigator.com/2011/10/28/judge-character/.

20. Nin, Anaïs. *The Diary of Anaïs Nin, 1939–1944.* Houghton Mifflin Harcourt, 1971, p. xiv.

21. Or, "If you treat an individual as he is, he will stay as he is, but if you treat him as if he were what he ought to be, and could be, he will become what he ought to be and could be."

Lifetime Speaker's Encyclopedia, "578." Edited by Jacob Morton Braude. Prentice-Hall, 1962, p. 69.

22. Lewis, C. S. *Mere Christianity.* Rough cut revised edition. HarperCollins, 2001, p. 32.

23. Proust, Marcel. *The Death of the Cathedrals.* Translated by Tim Newcomb. Newcomb Livraria Press, p. 26.

24. Lee, Harper. *To Kill a Mockingbird.* Dramatic Publishing Company, 1970, p. 76.

25. Pickering, Ellen. *Sir Michael Paulet.* T. C. Newby, 1842, p. 205.

This quotation is attributed widely to Cato, despite a lack of historical evidence. However, as it turns out, the quotation is (verifiably) a line in a nineteenth-century novel by Ellen Pickering.

26. Boetcker, *The Ten Cannots.*

27. Wilde, Oscar. *Lady Windermere's Fan.* 1892.

28. Brahms, Johannes. Quoted in John Eliot Gardiner, *Music in the Castle of Heaven.* Alfred A. Knopf, 2013.

29. Walters, Sam. "Yes, Galileo Actually Said That," *Discover.* February 20, 2023. https://www.discovermagazine.com/the-sciences/yes-galileo-actually-said-that.

Made in the USA
Middletown, DE
26 June 2024

56348732R00120